LOVE IS ALL THAT MATTERS

Walking through the fire

NANCY BELLE WOOD

A true story of one woman's journey of "Walking Through the Fire." Her survival of horrific child abuse and the devastating loss of her one true love. Her quest to heal and unify the broken child within her, with the woman of strength she had to become…the woman she was born to be.

Nancy Belle Wood <nancybelleblake@gmail.com>
Cover artwork: Bjarne Winkler <wecaptureyourbusiness@gmail.com>

TABLE OF CONTENTS

FOREWORD

I have been seeing Nancy as her therapist while she has been working on her personal Journey. I am a licensed clinical social worker in a private practice with over 30 years of experience. I have a specialization in the area of trauma. I am also certified as a Critical Incident First Responder. I go to work sites where employees are experiencing a trauma, done on a group and/or individual basis. Critical Incident Stress Debriefing (CISD) accelerates the rate of "normal recovery in normal people, who are having normal reactions to abnormal events."

This book, *Love is All That Matters*, is a very powerful story of a journey from grief to transition. Nancy lost the love of her life in a horrific accident, and this book describes her honest, personal and spiritual journey.

In this world, we often face very challenging situations. The reality is, in every crisis there is an opportunity for transformation. If we solely focus on how things appear in the gross physical world, we miss the deeper meaning of events in our lives.

Nancy expresses how one can and must "stay in the fire." People can often get frozen in the pain of how trauma affects their soul's physical layer. When we stay stuck in the physical level, in how and what happened, what should not have happened, or how things should be different, we suffer even more. It can be tempting to get stuck in "because" and shut down. *"Because I lost my husband, because I am alone, because life didn't turn out like I thought it was supposed to."* Nancy beautifully expresses how she learned to walk through the fire, learning the lessons, learning to stay in her present awareness and allowing the pain to be what it is.

What I find quite profound is Nancy, through her journey, trusted more and more her ability as an intuitive. This wonderful gift would come out in her many times in her hot tub, where it was like she could channel a higher wisdom coming through and supporting her in the journey. Channeling can be perceived as the ability to allow wisdom from our guides or helpers, or it can be channeling our higher power. Whatever the source, Nancy has the ability to connect with the wisdom working within her and guiding her on her journey.

We all have a deeper wisdom that is available for us to learn to use and trust. When we are able to, in times of what feels like unbearable pain, we can ask for guidance and if we are receptive to receiving it, we can realize we are not alone. It is easy to get blinded by seeing reality at a gross physical level. We all have gifts and a purpose. When we lose a loved one, it can require us to change what we see as our path and purpose. This book is about embracing the change, embracing the layers of pain as we go on the journey, and embracing a New Path forward, step by step. We are more, we have a soul that has wisdom, we in our Essence are light and love, yet we forget this. A Buddhist saying, "We don't want to suffer, but our misguided pursuit of happiness and stability that is based on impermanent pleasure, objects and people only leads to dissatisfaction." Living in a reactive manner to our thoughts can keep us on an unstable and emotional hamster type wheel and this can cause suffering. By being more aware and conscious, by moving beyond our thoughts, we can experience more of a state of peace.

This book is a very powerful guide for others who are stuck in their pain on how to work through the layers and experience them. These painful layers are telling us where to go in our journey. Nancy has a beautiful gift: the ability to do the work of transforming herself, and now her gift can be used for helping others with their story. Nancy, through her writing and her poems, is able to be a lighthouse, shining the light on how to transcend profound grief to the path of coming back home where we are light and love. We need a lighthouse to help us through the storm of grief. Allow Nancy to be that lighthouse for you through her connection of poetry as she connects with her soul. Once you do the work of your journey, you may also find the light you seek is within you, and you are now able to be a lighthouse for others. Thank you, Nancy, for sharing your gifts and your light with others battling through the journey of life with this moving and very honest and heartfelt book.

Elaine Westendorf, LCSW (Licensed Clinical Social Worker)

DEDICATION

This book is dedicated to my three children, Jenny, Chrissy, and Josh, and the daughter of my heart, Jamie. As well as my seven grandchildren, Destiny, Zander, Archer, Morgan, Karmen, Cameron, and Liam.

I cannot forget my loving support groups of women I am blessed to have in my life. The Ya Ya's and Soul Connection. They loved me through some of the hardest and most painful times of my life, always believing in me.

I have to thank Leslie, Tukey, Dave, and Suzanne for helping me with many details of this book. Also, my #1 Elf Bjarne for helping me with my cover and pictures, and still seeing the magic of Love.

Last of all, to my Husband, Jimmy. You taught me so much about Love and how to see the beauty of the backside of a waterfall.

This is a picture of my Ya Ya Sisters. Not everyone is in this picture, but everyone of them is dearly loved. We have been a support for each other for around 50 years. We helped each other through many of life's hardest struggles. Never judgment, only unconditional love. We are always welcoming to new Ya Ya's. You need only come once to become a part of us. I am so very blessed to have these women in my life.

Author's Notes

I started writing poetry when I was a teen. It was a way for my soul to cry and try to work out my crazy life. My poems are prayers. Some poems I work on, and some poems work on me. By that I mean they write themselves. Typically I have a problem, a feeling or a thought that won't leave me alone. When I find a space for my mind to rest (often my hot tub), the poems bubble out of me. If I don't get pen to paper instantly, they will be lost forever. It is like I am not writing the poems, more like I am taking dictation. They are a part of me and part of something more. More? I can't explain that in simple words. They feel like they are answers to prayer, full of wisdom I don't always feel I possess. Some say that I "channel" them. Could be. I'm open to that, but I don't know. What I know is that my poetry is a gift. It longs to be shared and given its own light of understanding and love. I'm not a big poetry fan, but my heart needed to find a way to express all the emotions and deep questions I had exploding out of me my whole life. I must explain, the grammar and punctuation in my poems drive some

Nancy Belle Wood

people crazy. To me, my poems have their own heartbeat. I use ellipses ("...") very often. Too much for some. An ellipsis is more than a comma. The dictionary states its meaning as, "A type of punctuation that represents a pause." That is exactly what "..." means to me. Stop and think about what you just read. Digest it in your mind. Ask yourself, "What does she mean?" My poems are also raw, gritty and real. I do not sugarcoat my words. My poems are not "nice," but they are honest. So when they speak, I have learned to listen to the teachers of my soul. It is my deepest wish they will speak to your soul too, share guidance and wisdom on your life's journey, and maybe give you some peace knowing you are heard and not alone.

Writing poetry is the means by which I can put my heart on paper. One of my poems says "I can bleed on paper, expose my soul and all of who I am in words." My poetry became a way for me to learn and grow through my life's lessons and help others along their way. Sometimes my poems can be a voice in the dark and a light at the end of a seemingly endless tunnel. My poems most often bubble out of me. I can hardly write quickly enough to jot them down. They are a mix of all my human emotions, and guidance from…God, the Universe, most definitely a Higher Power. I am blessed with this gift. Throughout this book I will share with you my journey through the death of my beloved Jimmy. Through my poems, my thoughts, and my lessons, I am constantly learning, growing, and becoming. I will speak my truth. I am no more special than anyone else, but I will share with you my biggest and most important lesson of all before you read my book…

Love is all that matters!

For nearly 10 years my husband and I were Mr. and Mrs. Claus Christmas morning for one of our local hospital. Bjarne Winkler was our photographer, he volunteered his gift of photography to the hospital, to capture these priceless moments in pictures for the families of these very sick children, who could not be home on Christmas. These moments spent with these dear children and families can't help but fill you with the true meaning of Christmas. I can honestly say, that for Mr. Claus, myself and our #1 Elf Bjarne these were some of the most important moments in our lives.

Chapter 1

A Real Love Story

Where to start? I guess as in all stories, you start at the beginning. Once upon a time…

No wait, this is no fairytale. Yet, it is a love story. One that has passed the test of time. We walked and sometimes ran through the maze of life, ever holding onto each other, come what may.

My beloved Jimmy. We dated one week, were engaged for six months, and married for 42 years. Just so you know, I don't recommend this for everyone, but it worked for us. When I first saw my Jimmy, for me it was love at first sight. I was 17 and a foster kid. To say I had a hard childhood is an understatement and someday I will write that book too, but for now this is the story of my beloved Jimmy and the power of Love that transcends even death.

We were both so young and he was very innocent in ways I was not. I was Jimmy's first kiss. I was a foster kid and grew up with sexual abuse and all that comes with it. So let's just say Jimmy was not my first kiss but he was my forever kiss.

In 2020, I lost my beloved Jimmy. On the very morning of his death he was joking around, telling me how he was going to outlive all of us because he was in better physical shape. It was his way of trying to remind me to take better care of myself. I have diabetes and am overweight. That always concerned him. He told me numerous times that if I died and left him

Jim and I got married December 10, 1977

here alone for twenty years, when he got to heaven, he would be really mad at me.

On January 5, 2020, by 2 p.m., my Jimmy had passed. He accidentally electrocuted himself in our backyard while working on a wood burning project and I came home to find him. The site of my beloved is still excruciating to recall. I suffer from PTSD due to the trauma of finding my Jimmy.

I don't want to share the gruesome details of what I saw. Frankly, no one should see what I saw. How First Responders do it, I really don't know, but I am grateful for them. I was home alone when I discovered my Jimmy. I was in total shock and ran to him in disbelief. I wanted to help him in any way I could, but it was clear he had passed. He was gone. As I ran to him to see if he could possibly still be alive, I could hear him speak in my head, yes my dead husband spoke to me. In a deafening yell, "UNPLUG ME!" It was then I realized that the electricity was still running through him and if I were to touch him, it would run through me. I ran to the plug and pulled it. Then I stood there looking at what was left of my husband. I called 911. As I waited in the middle of the road for the police to arrive, I found myself screaming. Trying to flag down the police who had gone to the front of my house, not the back where I was with my Jimmy. I had a fleeting thought, if I kept screaming, I would end up with the migraine from hell. That thought quickly vanished into pure, unrelenting Soul pain as the reality of the situation started to sink in. This is where I started my "Walk through the Fire."

I called my children and everyone gathered. We were at the neighbor's house in their yard. My beloved home now was a crime scene. I knew Jimmy hadn't meant to electrocute himself, but the police still had to make sure there was no foul play. All my heart knew was that he was gone and even though he was gone, he still protected me. "UNPLUG ME!" he screamed in my ears. Even in death, he kept watch over me.

I will share with you my journey through grief, or as I like to call it, "Walking Through the Fire." I have had a lot of loss in my life, a lot of pain, and a lot of experiences no one should have to deal with. Despite all of this, the loss of my Jimmy was the hardest thing I have ever had to endure. Harder than the terror of my childhood beatings, hunger, abandonment, and nightly rapes.

I have learned many things in these last two years. It is my hope and wish that my journey through this pain and grief… "Walking Through the Fire," will help you walk through your own Fire. I was given the gift of being able to put into words deep pain and anguish. It is my deepest prayer that what my poems truly say resonates with you as you walk your own journey so you don't feel so alone.

Growing up, I had to be a survivor, it was survival of the fittest. I learned to read people and emotions. That is the gift my childhood gave me. I want you to know I'm not complaining about my childhood. It was a hard road but I really like "me" and I wouldn't be "me" if I hadn't learned the lessons that my childhood taught me. Would I want to do it again? Hell no! But like I said, I wouldn't be the "me" I am today without those life lessons.

The first night after my husband passed, I walked around like a zombie. I was in shock. Shock from the fact that he was gone forever and shock from what I saw and could not share with anyone. Images flashed in my head constantly. Although my three children are grown, I knew they too were hurting and there were the grandkids to consider. My mind was, as you would expect, a blur of this memory or that one, what should have been, but never will be, along with the horror I had witnessed and knew I could never unsee. I was doing my best to act whatever was so called "normal" for a woman who had just lost her husband of 42 years, whatever that was. But apparently, I was failing at this. Later, the kids told me I was acting like the dog who was easily distracted by squirrels in the movie "UP." In other words, I could not focus and was easily distracted. The fake smile I had plastered on my face was fooling no one.

At about 8:30 the evening of his passing, my son came to me and very tenderly told me I needed to go to bed. Bed! Was he kidding? All my kids were gathered in the living room, I really just wanted to be with them. I asked him if I was driving them nuts, he said, "Yes." In my zombie state, I got myself some hot tea, and stood at the doorway to "Our" bedroom. I said to my now dead husband, "Looks like it's you and me now, Honey." Our bedroom was more his space than mine. It was his space to watch TV and recharge. There were also times when depression hit my husband sometimes for days. He would close the door and stay in the dark under the covers.

Putting on a new pair of "Big Girl Panties," I stepped into the room. It was a very long, sleepless night with many more to follow. It was the beginning of my life all over again.

I was in shock for over a month. I remember bits and pieces from the weeks that followed. I remember a few days after my Jimmy passed, on the kitchen table, I found a note written from my grandson Archer to Papa. It said… *"hi papa I Just wanted you to know that granma is good She has friends comeing over and there telling stroies she getting gifts. from archer to papa"*

For me to wake up and find that beautiful handwritten, misspelled note from my grandson to his papa, helped me know that my husband's presence was still here and present in all our lives, and would be forever!

A day after my Jimmy passed, my son and his two boys moved in with me. My husband and I have been very close with our two grandsons. Having them move in was a blessing. The first school day after my husband passed, Zander, my older grandson, was having a hard time dealing with his papa's passing. He hadn't cried and all of it was very overwhelming for him. He looked at me that morning as he was getting ready for school and said, "Grandma, can I stay home and mourn my kitties?" Zander had always felt very close to cats and often they seem to be his "Love Language." He didn't have words or understand how to mourn for his papa, so this is what came out of my sweet boy that morning. I held him close and said, "Well, we have to ask your dad, but it sounds okay to me." His dad looked at me to make sure it was okay. I nodded. Then my son said,

This the note my grandson Archer wrote that I found on my kitchen table a few mornings after Papa died.

"Well Zander, if you stay home with Grandma, I have a lot of things to do and I need you to know this is not video time. If you stay home from school, you will help Grandma with anything she needs and help take care of her when I am not here. If that's okay with you, yes, you can stay home and mourn your kitties."

That day was a hard day for me and I was emotionally worn out and exhausted. I wasn't the playful Grandma Zander was used to. I stayed in bed that day and honestly must have looked pretty messed up to my poor Zander. (Frankly, I was messed up!) My bedroom door was open and every time he walked by, I would smile and ask him if he needed anything. He would answer, "No." I noticed he walked by quite often. I called him into my room and said, "Are you checking on your Grandma?" He said, "Yes." I told him, "You can come in anytime you want. Grandma's just sad and missing Papa, but I will be okay again. Today is just a hard day for me." Then my sweet boy said, "Grandma, do you want me to draw you a Dragon?" I said, "Well yes, I would love for you to draw me a Dragon." So Zander settled down and took a lot of time and drew a beautiful Dragon for me. As I looked over his beautiful Dragon, he said, "Grandma my Dragon is going to protect you for Papa!" I told him how much I loved it, that his artwork was wonderful, and I would frame it. He asked me if I wanted him to draw another one. I said, "Yes! I do! I need a whole flock

My grandson Zander drew both these next two pictures of dragons. He drew them to protect me for Papa.

of them!" He said, "Grandma, they are not called a flock; they are called a Wing." I laughed and said, "Yes, I need a whole 'Wing' of them!" He promptly sat down and drew several more. To this day, both Archer's note to Papa and my Wing of Dragons adorn my walls. They are a constant reminder I am loved and protected, that I have the best grandkids in the world, and how blessed I really am.

These 3 young men are my son's boys. Zander, {right to left} Liam, and Archer.
I love these boys!

Chapter 2

Jimmy's Service

We had a wonderful outside service for my Jimmy on his beloved soccer field. At least 500 people came. I hugged so many people that day. At the beginning of his service, we played the song he had sung and recorded at his brother's little studio for our 35th anniversary. My three children even stood together as our daughter Jenny spoke. Probably my husband's proudest moment. I even spoke at his service and shared a little about my Jimmy.

"Thank you all for coming, to honor my Jimmy. Let me tell you about the man I met, before all of you did. I had first seen Jimmy at the recreation center where I worked. I was 17 and a foster kid. He was 22 and Oh, so handsome! They were picking teams for softball, which I had never played before. But Jimmy was one of the coaches so I went, and...he didn't pick me. But within a few days he saw the error in his thinking and traded for me. So, like many of you, he was my first coach too.

A lot of 'STUFF' happened in my childhood, not good, and I carried that pain literally. I had the transcripts from a court hearing I took with me, from move to move. I privately called it my 'Anti-Bible,' like a dark heavy weight upon my heart. Well, Jimmy decided I'd held on to that pain long enough. He said, 'Follow me.' I had no idea where he was going, but I started to follow without the transcripts and he said, 'Grab those.' I did. I followed him with transcripts in hand to the trash cans. He said, 'Pick up the lid,' I hesitated. He said, 'Pick, Up, The, Lid!' I did. He said, 'Now throw that in there.' I hesitated again. He looked at me and said, 'That is Not who you are!' I put them inside the trash can. Then he said, 'Put the lid on. I don't want to hear about this again.' Never once did he use any of that stuff against me, or throw it in my face. He never mentioned it again. That's the kind of man my Jimmy was.

Jimmy's legacy can live on in all of you too. By reminding us all, we too, may have held onto pain for too long. It is not who we are. He always joked, because I was a foster kid, that he was my last placement, my 'Forever Home.' He will always be my heart. He was far from perfect, as we all are. The joke is, now he gets to be perfect, and I can't interrupt him anymore.

I want you to know, I was his first Starfish, and will forever be his 'Giggly Bride.'

My Jimmy was well known for all the little stories he would share with his teams at each practice. Each story had a meaning and something to teach. One story he was particularly known for sharing was the story of the little child who found many Starfishes washed up on the sand after a storm. The child started throwing them back into the ocean knowing if they stayed on the sand they would die. Someone yelled to the child, 'You can't save them all. It will not make any difference. You're wasting your time.' As he threw in another Starfish, the child yelled back, 'It made a difference to that one.' That story was told at his service by a young woman he once coached. As the young people spoke, they often shared how they could relate to the story of the Starfish, and how Jimmy's words of encouragement and the time he spent with them had made a difference in their lives.

It was a beautiful service, filled with many children, some, now adults, he had coached in soccer and other sports over a course of almost 30 years. He was a youth mentor in many ways; through church youth groups, CASA (Court Appointed Special Advocate for foster kids) and ATOU (A Touch of Understanding, a Disability Awareness Program). I cannot forget, he was also Santa. He was asked to be Santa at the CASA Christmas Party one year for the foster kids. He told them, "Only if I can bring Mrs. Claus." We were Mr. and Mrs. Claus for nearly ten years. Each year we were asked to do more and more events. I was truly in heaven. Truth be told, Jimmy was shy, and Santa took some getting used to for him. He loved the one-on-one time with the kids and parents, but being in the spotlight in a big crowd was beyond his comfort level. Luckily for him, he had Mrs. Claus (Me!) and she was always the biggest kid in the room.

Grandkids at the service for their Papa,(right to left) Archer, back row, Destiny, next to her in the back row with the pink hat on is our Morgan. In Destiny's arms is her sister Karmen, and next to her their brother Cameron. They are all wearing Manchester United soccer uniforms. Papa's favorite team.

In the days, weeks, months, and even years since Jimmy's passing, I have learned a lot about myself. I have learned a lot about pain. It is an incredible teacher. Also, Love is the only thing that really matters. Love is like a double-edged sword. To truly love is to risk it all. I am a firm believer in Love. Yes, with Love can come deep sorrow. There is no question about it, as my story will tell. I can tell you with all my Soul, Love is what saved me.

Chapter 3
Home

This is where my story of "Walking through the Fire" begins.

Forty-two years of marriage. We had just gotten our trailer and were ready for retirement. Our time. We were so excited to travel and camp our way across our beautiful United States. See all the things we never had time or extra money to see. Relax and just enjoy each other's company. Reconnect with each other.

But in a flash it was all gone.

Dreams, hopes, wishes, all vanished. My future vanished. It was now being rewritten. I was alone. Yes, I had grown kids, grandkids, and friends. But my heart was gone. Nothing seemed right. I was alone in a world full of people. In many ways, I felt buried alive. One foot in heaven, one foot on earth. To my surprise, the world moved on. I was stuck living in my own private hell. Nothing was right, everything was wrong. My world was upside down. Not even my home felt like my home.

Home

"Home" to some a simple word,
something they have always had.
For me "Home" was always destroyed,
whenever my world went bad.

The dictionary says,

"A place where one lives permanently,
as a member of a family."
My reality was more often than not,
one of refugee.

But for 42 years…
I had a real home.
Three children we raised,
the greatest love I had known.

Yet once again my world blew up,
my beloved husband has died.
No longer do we walk this earth,
hand in hand and side by side.

I know the drill…
survive at all cost.
But shattered is my home,
and I am so lost.

What is next? I wait for more,
I will survive, it's what I do.
When life leaves you little choice,
you would too.

I've seen the signs, "Home Sweet Home."
My heart sees them like a joke.
My stomach wants to vomit,
my throat begins to choke.

Slowly I start to realize…
I still have a roof and four walls,
and no "Wolf" banging at the door.
I know, this is my wakeup call.

I have lost my beloved…
yet I still have a home.
And it's full of memories,
of the greatest love I've known.

I am safe, I was loved,
I am grateful for my life.
I miss you, Honey…
I loved being your wife.

Thank you for my home,
and the safe place in your heart.
I can still feel your love,
even though we're apart.

Know I am more grateful,
than you will ever know.
I will honor our love,
and try to thrive and grow.

I still have a Home,
I am safe, and I am strong.
"Home Sweet Home"
will be my heart's new song.

The reality is,
this is so hard for me.
For in my heart,
you and me, is all I really see.

We will meet again,
for your heart is my real home.
I miss you my love…
You're the only home I have ever known.

My Jimmy in a hollowed out big tree. Jim loved camping, and hiking, and anything to do with the great outdoors.

Chapter 4

The Glove

I don't believe in coincidence. Everything happens for a reason. That being said, I will share with you a couple of things that happened at this time of my life.

My Jimmy could be an "Odd Duck" from time to time. He collected single gloves he found that people lost. (I still have a small box of them.) He thought it was such a waste to let a perfectly good glove get thrown away when he could find another glove for the other hand. Logical to him. A few days before he passed, he stuck one of his old ugly gloves on a stick in the yard making the sign language sign for "I Love You." He was so proud of himself. I couldn't see anything but one of the dirty gloves he was always picking up. I insisted it come down claiming it was not "Art." He said simply, "I like it, so it stays." I walked away but thought to myself, it won't last.

A few days later he passed, and I forgot about that beautiful glove in my yard. The first time I drove my car around the back of our house, there in the road not 10 feet from where my Jimmy passed, was a bright red glove. I smiled and said out loud, "I love you too, Honey!" Then, as I pulled up in front of our house, I remembered his glove he so proudly put on display in our yard days before. I walked into our yard, looked straight at his beautiful glove on display signing, "I Love You," for all the world to see. With a smile on my face and tears in my eyes, I said, "Ok Jimmy, it can stay." I could see his cute crooked smile shining back at me. He had won. His message was clear, for me to remember he loved me.

The other story I wanted to share is a bit out there, but I swear to you it is true. In the many years of our marriage, my Jimmy's feet put many, many holes in our sheets. Brand new ones too! He couldn't help it, and never even knew he was doing it. I would patch them and tell him frustratedly, I had just gotten these sheets and he would have to deal with the stiff patch at his feet.

A few months after he passed, I was missing him so much. It might sound silly, but I had some people asking me if he visited me at night, or if I saw him, or if he touched me. I said, "No." He knew better than to scare me, but he spoke with me constantly. This particular night, I asked him to come into my dreams (if I could sleep). To my surprise, I awoke that morning with my foot in a hole in my sheets! I had just put brand new sheets on the night before. Yet when I pulled back the covers to see the bottom of the sheet on my side of the bed, it was all torn up. Just the way my Jimmy had done so many times before. But this time, it was on My side. Again, message received. My Jimmy was with me, as he always has been. The veil between us was thin. I had never torn sheets before and have not once since that night. No, he didn't touch me. No, I did not see a ghost. He knew that would scare me. The sheets, well, he knew I would know it was him. He got a good laugh out of it, I am sure. I knew when I shared this story with friends, it would be suspect, "The poor grieving Widow." I took a picture, but many people have explanations that have nothing to do with my Jimmy. I get it, they don't understand. How could they? So much of everything I had been experiencing they could not understand. But I swear to you, it is true.

This glove still sits in my yard today, reminding me of how much my Hubby loved his life.

CHAPTER 5

SNOWGLOBE

As I start to write this book, I remember how everything in my world had changed. I was in shock. Shock from the sight of my beloved Jimmy, burning. But also from my world being turned upside down. Nothing was right. Even simple mundane things I took for granted had changed. Normal things had changed too, like I couldn't read. My mind could not focus. Even now, two years later, I can't sit down and read a book. My taste buds changed. The tea I had to have first thing in the morning for over 40 years, no matter what, tasted disgusting to me. My mind couldn't rest. Thoughts ran around inside me chasing their own tails, in an endless circle. There was no rest, no peace, only indescribable pain. Some say I was numb, and while it may have looked that way, I was anything but numb.

I was in the hot tub, my place of peace and prayer. I was thinking about how to explain this time in my life so you could honestly walk this journey with me. A snowglobe came to my mind. Inside this beautiful snowglobe was my life, my world, my friends, my family. Everyone but me. Jimmy had passed. Plans were being made. Friends gathered. I could see them all, like looking in a snowglobe. But I was outside looking in. My shadow was inside the globe. I knew everything that was going on. I even participated. But my real world was black. I walked around like a ghost in my own life. No one knew my grief, my pain. I was someone to be managed and moved around. Some kind people told me they even "knew" how I felt, they had lost a parent. I bluntly told them they had no idea how I felt, and feel; I hoped they never would know this pain. I found I had little patience or filter. Reality was crashing down my door. I was alone. Alone in a world filled with people I loved, and who loved me. But I was terrifyingly alone. I was outside of the glass globe that had been my life, looking in, knowing nothing would ever be the same again.

Change has never been my friend. Change meant uncertainty, fear, and pain. I much prefer the simplicity of everyday life. Some call it mundane; I call it peace. To me, my world had just blown to bits and I was caught in the blast with all my skin torn off. Everything hurt and the fact that I was still living was a cruel joke. I was not, nor have I ever been suicidal. But have no doubt, I was pissed that I was still alive. It was one of the very few times I was angry I was a survivor. I had survived horrible things in my past, and I was proud of who I had become, despite my Life's Journey, or as I have come to learn, who I am because of my Life's Journey and the choices I made. I have found pain is an incredible teacher, but only if you are willing to face the pain and see it for what it truly is, Love. That being said, I do understand, not all pain is caused by Love, but pain still teaches something and it doesn't have to be hate.

Kissing Santa Claus. A very favorite picture of mine.

Chapter 6

Journal

I went to New Hampshire to my brother and sister-in-law's house after the service for Jimmy. I was there for a month. I needed to grieve, but I couldn't hurt my children, and I couldn't hide my pain. (Though they were all grown, what I had seen was not for their eyes or ears.) No matter how hard I tried to be strong, I couldn't be strong for them and for me.

While I was with my brother and his beautiful wife, I just focused on myself. My sister-in-law took great care of me. She made sure I ate and gave me both the space I needed and someone to talk with. Along with my brother's unconditional love, kindness, and strong arms, I was in the best of care.

I tried to journal about my feelings, but this lasted only a few days. Poetry is my soul's real voice, but this is what I wrote.

"Monday, February 17th

And now my recovery begins… I'm sitting in bed sipping hot tea, listening to Indian flute music, in my New Hampshire home, my refuge. Last month on January 5th, my husband of forty-two years died suddenly. He accidentally electrocuted himself in my backyard. I found him burning. Oh, how I love that man. He was, and always will be my heart. I am a strong woman, I have survived and thrived in some horrible situations no one should ever have to live through. But I did, and I will survive this too, although this is the hardest one yet. Oh, I miss him so! He was always there, always my protector, my biggest fan, my love. I'm looking for a peaceful place in my mind to rest, my heart, to breathe, to let go, and to release the stress that plagues my body. I am in Survivor Mode. I've been here before but not in forty-two years. Now I'm sixty and my heart is broken. I know I will go on, it's what I do. But I refuse to be a shell of who I am. I need to grow, and even thrive in this barren land of my soul. I need to honor our life, and my own. I have always grown where life has planted me, wherever the "Winds of Life" blew me. I will again, my choice is clear. But I know living, surviving is not enough. I must thrive. I will become my best self. I will show the power of love in my life. Out of the ashes of my life I will rise again, for I am not dead. I am a survivor. Slowly I will rise and become an even better version of myself. I will breathe in life and all its gifts. I will not be bitter or angry or live in this sadness forever. I cannot. I am strong, not because I am any different from anyone else, but because in life you have choices and I choose to live. I am a survivor not because I am brave, but because I can't live in this pain, in the sadness, forever. It would be a living death. Who could truly live in "Poor me?" I have been so sad, I have been depressed, but that is no life. Life is a gift, and I choose to count my blessings and be grateful. So as I climb out of this grave, of the deepest heartbreak and sadness I have ever known, I will be kind to myself. I will breathe. I will rest for the climb back to my new life and all the treasures it will hold. When I stumble and fall, and I will, I will reach again for the higher ground, 'till I can feel the sun's warmth again and the true warmth of a hug, 'till my eyes see more than pain and darkness. In a way, it's life's rebirth, not of my choosing, but a gift no less. There is life outside this pain and this unbelievable sadness. I will find my feet again and I will stand. I will laugh again. But for now I climb slowly, and reach for the sunlight.

So sad...

I miss you...I miss your smile, your kisses goodnight on the cheek. I miss the sound of your voice, your breathing next to me at night...

I just miss you..."

I pampered myself with two beautiful massages while I was in New Hampshire. I was a hot mess to say the least when I went to this beautiful, kind woman. I explained to her the first time, I was grieving the love of my life of forty-two years. I didn't need to say more. Her massage massaged my very soul. Her hands worked on my body; her spirit and energy worked on my soul. For a time, she let my pain rest. Later, I found out she was studying to be a nurse. She wasn't afraid to feel my pain and share her love. Her touch did both. I told her she would be a wonderful nurse. I could see how blessed the patients would be under her care. I sure was. She helped my body and mind prepare to come home to California.

This is a picture of Jim and I when we were younger. Oh how I love this man.

James Patrick Wood

CHAPTER 7
THE BEGINNING

Remember how I spoke of the day my Jimmy passed and I was screaming in the middle of the road as I waited for the police? Even in my shock and immense grief, I knew I would get a horrible migraine…but I didn't! Four days before I was to fly home, to my surprise, my brain turned on. I called it "coming online." Like a computer, my brain was waking me up. First, I woke with a horrible migraine, but only in the back third of my head. I could hear my brain asking me, "How are you doing? Can you handle this?" I remember kind of laughing, and answering, "It sucks, but I'm ok." I nursed the one third of my aching brain that day. By the end of the day, it was not perfect, but it was better. The next morning the middle of my brain came on with a vengeance. Again, my brain asked me, "So, how are you doing today? Can you handle it?" By now, I realized what was happening. My brain had protected me from dealing with this pain for months. Don't get me wrong, I was in agony with grief, but my body had held the migraines off. It was now time to wake up and deal with life as well as grief. So, the next morning, again I woke with a migraine from hell. My brain had awakened in three sections, one section each of the three mornings before I left. The body is an amazing machine. I already had felt overwhelmed when Jimmy passed and my body knew it might have broken me if I had to deal with even more pain. My body was preparing me for the real world and going home to my new "Normal" life as a single woman.

Before I left my brother's house I wrote this poem.

The Beginning

I was dead, buried with my beloved,
Yet I still walk this earth alone.
How could he be gone, my beloved of 42 years?
He was my home.

My safe place, my heart,
my strength, my shield.
The pain is overwhelming,
but still, I must yield.

He pulled me up,
from the ashes of my childhood.
Wrapped in his arms,
I thrived and stood.

He didn't see the filth around me.
He said "It's not who you are."
To him I was the sunshine,
and the first evening star...

Somehow he saw,
with the eyes of his Soul.
And in his light,
I grew strong and whole.

This time I stand alone,
in the ashes of my life,
and learn to live again,
not being Jimmy's wife.

I know he'll never leave me,
but this journey is for me alone.
I need to stand up strong...
and build my own home.

I am still alive,
though how I do not know...
My journey is yet to be.
Somehow I'll thrive and grow.

My legs are unsteady.
They buckle when I stand.
But I can hear him calling…
"Come on Hon, take my hand."

This path before me,
will light as I go.
Inch by inch,
I will thrive and grow.

Who are you…
if not Jimmy's wife?
Inch by inch I'll step forward,
and embrace this new life.

For I am yet alive…
as the dawn breaks on a new day.
"Don't waste it, Hon!"
I can hear him say.

I came home to California, trying to put this new life of mine together one day at a time. I went right into survivor mode. I painted the whole outside of the house. Sometimes I was outside with a flashlight painting. Anything to avoid going to bed, or thinking, or feeling. I was holding my "Big Girl Panties" on with suspenders, and they were torn to shreds. I was torn to shreds…I worked in the yard, 'till I was bruised and bleeding. I laid heavy pavers, moved rocks and dirt, and brought home over 100 bags of bark. The whole time I worked, I could hear Jimmy talking to me. He was the voice in my head constantly, suggesting I do it this way or that way. "Use this tool, not that one." I found myself having conversations with him, only I talked out loud, he talked in my head.

COVID had made its deadly mark on us all, day by day getting worse. Everyone stayed away. Truth be told, I was awful company anyway. I was angry, but not at anyone, just angry he was gone, and I was alone.

26

I trudged on, putting on a fake smile when I could. But my eyes could never lie. I was broken, from the inside out. Running on a hamster wheel going nowhere, really fast.

Some days were really hard, and I struggled just to get out of bed. But each day was a new beginning and a new chance to live this new life of mine. I tried to keep busy. I tried to say, "Yes" to different opportunities that came my way even if I didn't feel quite up to it. From time to time I could even feel the warmth of the sunshine once again. This next poem I wrote while learning to stand again.

CHAPTER 8
WALKED AMONG THE LIVING

Day One

Today I walked among the living,
breathing air into this new life.
I'm learning to live again,
being more than someone's wife.

Although he walks beside me,
he cannot hold my hand.
It's time for me to be bold,
to rise and to stand.

As I embrace the path before me,
I breathe in new air.
I do not walk alone,
in my heart, I know you're there.

Forever my champion,
my heart and my soul.
Somehow through healing,
I'm creating a new whole.

For shattered has my heart been,
broken to its core.
But I am picking up the pieces,
scattered on the floor.

And I am putting the pieces back,
one piece at a time.
I'll create a beautiful mosaic,
out of this heart of mine.

For I still have,
a life to live…
and so much love,
in this soul to give.

It is my heart's,
greatest prayer,
that all I love,
know how much I care.

That when the light,
From their hearts shine…
they see this beautiful,
heart of mine.

For it is only a reflection,
of all the love I've known,
and all the lessons learned,
and all the times I've grown.

I tried and I tried but my heart was broken. The feeling of loneliness was so overwhelming sometimes that no matter what I did, I was in pain, agonizing pain. The silence in my home was deafeningly loud. I couldn't sleep and when I did, I just dreamt. My dreams were all over the place as all my thoughts had been. In one of my dreams, I dreamed that Jimmy and I were going camping. We had sold our camper because of gas prices and went back to tent camping. My Jimmy was so excited we were going camping! The smile on his face was so big as he rubbed his hands together, filled with excitement, like the little boy I remember inside of him. To him camping was like Christmas morning. He said to me, "There's a yard sale over there, maybe they have a mattress pad for our bed." I told him I'd go check since it was a friend of mine having the yard sale. Maybe they would give me a good deal. Jimmy always loved a good deal. I went to the yard sale and asked my friend if she had a queen size mattress pad for Jimmy and me to use camping. All of a sudden in my dream there were all kinds of eyes looking at me, sad eyes, pity-filled eyes. I could hear them whispering, "Poor Dear, she may never be okay." My friend said, "I have a twin mattress pad that I could sell you." I said, "Oh dear, I need a queen so it will fit both Jimmy and me." Again all those sad eyes and the whispering words. Then my friend said, "You don't need a queen, Dear. Jimmy's gone." Then I woke up. For those few moments, I could remember the feeling of his joy and of the joy I had being with him. Yet, in an instant it was gone, reality came crashing back, but for those few moments, he was smiling again and I was not alone.

I was so lonely and I missed him. I knew there had to be a reason for my life, a reason why I was still here. But it felt like I was bleeding constantly from my Soul and I would never be the same again.

Jim walking across a fallen tree. One of his favorite things to do.

Chapter 9
Bleeding From my Soul

I Bled Today

I bled today…
from the gaping wound within my soul.
Bleeding where I once
was whole.

Lonely, I am so lonely.
I weep in tears of blood.
So many tears, so much blood,
I'm drowning in the flood.

How long?
How long must I die?
Over and over,
my soul wants to cry.

I walk in this world unseen.
No need to hide.
Walking amongst the living,
as though I, myself, have died.

So much to live for.
So much joy.
Yet I feel a puppet…
or Fates cruelest toy.

Alive, yet dead,
in the deepest parts of me.
A cruel twist of fate,
is all that I can see.

I'm broken.
Scattered all around.
I tried to put the pieces back...
at least the ones I found.

But they don't seem to fit,
I'm not "me" anymore.
I'm battered and broken,
scattered on the floor.

I don't want to be a new me.
I liked who I was.
I used to laugh and sing all day,
simply just because.

Now tears fall, and fall, and fall,
I can't find my way free.
I'm tired of this pain,
I need to find me.

And every time I hear me call,
I find I bleed some more.
And I find my broken self,
shattered on the floor.

"Honey, I love you!
But I've got to let you go."
But pain envelopes me...
You're all I really know.

My safe place, my home,
my shelter from the storm.
And now, there is nothing...
that is my new Norm.

I am strong,
I've always had to be.
But I hated life before you,
when there was only me.

And I don't want to return to that.
I was so alone.
I didn't even know what it was like,
to have a home.

I know I will persevere.
It's what I've always done.
But now my soul cries out in pain,
"Run! Run! Run!"

Run until it goes away.
Run before you're caught!
But reality is screaming...
"My Dear, It's Time You Fought!"

"Fight?" I scream!
"It's all I've done since the day I was born!"
But I guess that's what I'm doing,
every time that I mourn.

Dear God, I miss you so much,
my pain is All of Me.
And I can't begin to see,
the me I used to be.

A new "Me" will awaken...
A new birth of my Soul.
And somehow I'll emerge again,
once again whole.

Change is inevitable.
A new "Me" will emerge.
And just like a new book,
I'll be filled with new words.

My story is yet unwritten,
sands of time, are yet to fall.
But Darling, I want you to know…
I loved you most of all.

Though yet I walk this path alone,
please help me feel you near.
And any time I need you,
please help me know you're there.

I know we'll walk together again…
but today I walk alone.
Know this my beloved,
you are the greatest love I've known.

I remember the day I wrote this last poem. I stayed up all night crying, bleeding from my Soul. It didn't seem possible my Jimmy was gone, and I was still here. The world kept revolving. The sun rose and the sun set. People laughed at the stupidest stuff. Everything I used to love was repulsive to me now. I was broken. Somehow I needed to find my place in this new world and frankly, I wasn't sure I wanted to. How could God have taken him and not me too? I didn't want to be alone, and alone was all I was.

I could put a smile on and fake it for a while if I tried really hard. Deep down, I knew I was beyond blessed. I had a beautiful life. We didn't have much but we had each other, our three children, and our beautiful grandchildren. I knew what it was like to be loved and a lot of people never get to know that. So, I began to struggle with how blessed I was, and how heartbroken I was at the same time. Two emotions that seem to repel each other were my world. How could I be so sad and also so blessed? But life comes in layers, and it is possible to be terribly sad and so grateful at the same time. I might not have a lot, but I have enough and for that I was very grateful. This time was very hard for me. I felt like I was betraying all the gifts I was given in my life, because I was so horribly sad. So this is how this next poem came to be.

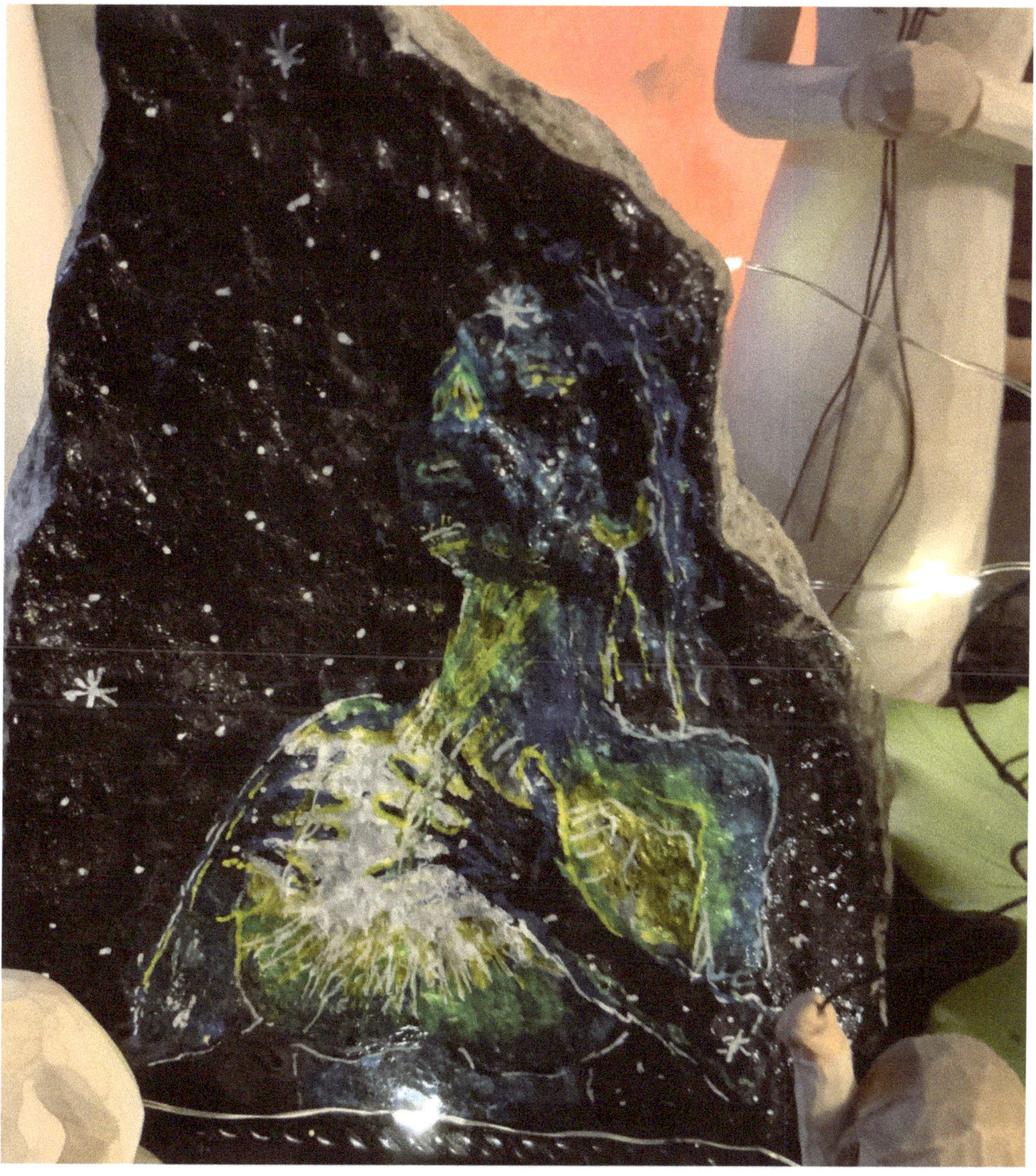

I found a picture of this rock on Pinterest, and I painted this one myself. To me my very soul is ablaze with both grief and love.

Chapter 10
Beyond Blessed

Before sharing this next poem I'm going to tell you about the moments just before I found my husband that horrible morning. I had been thrift store shopping, picking up this or that, nothing all that important. But I had found a new doormat for our porch that my Jimmy had just finished fixing. It seemed the perfect adornment to my beautiful new porch and summarized how I felt about our life together. The doormat said "Beyond Blessed" and I was. I knew how lucky I was to have found the life I had. I was Blessed! Moments after I placed that mat on the porch in front of our door I walked in the house and found my husband in the backyard. Everything had changed in my life in an instant, but I knew I was still Beyond Blessed. That mat still sits at the foot of my door. Yes, it is a constant reminder of finding my husband, but it is also a constant reminder of how blessed I am to have the life I do. I have had friends offer to take it away so it won't remind me of that day, but I need that mat. I need to be reminded of the full meaning of what that mat says. Yes, I found my husband minutes after I put that mat down, but it also reaffirmed that day and reaffirms today, my beautiful life and how very blessed I am.

Sad and Blessed

Who would have thought,
you could be both sad and blessed.
They are both gifts,
in my emotional treasure chest.

So much to be grateful for,
and to my core I am.
But the sadness fills my heart,
so, I find myself in that jam.

I lost the love of my life,
and in so many ways, my very soul.
I struggle to be happy,
and find my new whole.

Yet around every corner,
I see all the joys in my life.
And I know I am so much more,
than being Jimmy's wife.

God gave me gifts a plenty,
and so many still to love.
Somehow I need to go on,
even though my heart's above.

I want so much more,
than to make do and survive.
I want to be grateful…
I am still alive.

Yet I am so sad,
and I can't stop the tears.
But know I am grateful,
for all our years.

I miss talking with you,
about everything.
I miss hearing your voice,
as you'd hum or you'd sing.

I miss your hugs,
and soft pecks on the cheek.
I miss your advice,
the wise words you would speak.

I miss watching you with the grandkids,
and the silly things you'd do,
from "Pull my finger" to a tent in the house.
All of that was you.

It's hard to think,
I walk alone.
Your heart has always been,
my home.

Yet I know how blessed I was,
to be your wife.
And how blessed I am,
to have the gift of life.

But I am so lonely,
and I weep for what could have been.
But I know in my heart,
we will meet again.

So, for now…
I'll let the tears fall where they may.
And brace myself…
for a brand new day.

This is the rug I placed on my porch just before I found my beloved burning.
It is forever a reminder of how very Blessed I am everyday.

Chapter 11

Daddy

I have always struggled with meditation. I have a sort of monkey brain. It does what it wants to do, when it wants to do it. I know I'm supposed to be in charge of this brain, but trust me, it's like my tongue when I go to the dentist, it does its own thing. But there are times when I feel very connected to God, to the Universe, to more. But those moments happen without words and are truly just a gift to me. Often, they are not explainable in mere words. There have been several different experiences where I have been touched by the Universe. I don't talk about them often because, well, to others they won't make sense. I seem to look foolish in their eyes. But, I tell you from the bottom of my heart, it is real to me. One of these experiences happened when I was a little girl. It was two days before my 13th birthday. My beloved father, who was by no means perfect, but was my everything, was having an operation. He suddenly had a heart attack on the operating table and died. I was in my favorite music class. All of a sudden I felt him speak to my heart. I can give it words but in truth there were none. But I knew he was gone. His last words to my heart were, "It's going to be hard, but you're going to be ok." I put my head down and cried and cried and cried. My daddy was gone. The teacher came to me and asked me what was wrong. I told her "My daddy just died." she said, "But dear, you were fine five minutes ago." I said, "I know, but my daddy just died." I have no logical explanation for how I knew my daddy had just died, but I knew it without a doubt.

I was not aware at the time, but my mother had been in and out of mental institutions her whole life and had six children already taken from her. My three younger siblings and I were her last litter. (Later in life that became my little joke.) But, I did know my mother was not a "normal" mother. When my dad was alive, I always went to him and avoided her at all cost.

Later that day when I got out of school, my uncle came to pick me up, but I was not allowed to be around him. He was my mother's brother, and later I found out, most likely the father of my mother's first child. When we first moved to California from Boston, I had a sleepover at his and his wife's house and he put his hands down my pants. I made an excuse to leave and go to the bathroom. I brought the phone and the long cord into the bathroom and called my daddy. He told me to lock the door and not to come out of that room until I heard his voice. He came immediately to get me. Later, I could hear him yelling at my mom, telling her to keep her crazy relatives away from his children! Until the day my daddy died, I had not seen my uncle again.

But here he was, picking me up and I told him, "I'm not supposed to be around you!" He said my mother was in the car and she had something very sad to tell me. I already knew. Daddy had told me himself! So, my plan was, if I didn't see Mom in the car I would make a run for it. But Mom was there, a puddle in the front seat of the car. I climbed in the back, a very brave young girl. I told her she didn't need to tell me, I already knew daddy died. I told her that I would tell my three younger siblings, not her. That day, I became the parent. On my 13th birthday, two days after he died, my Daddy was buried.

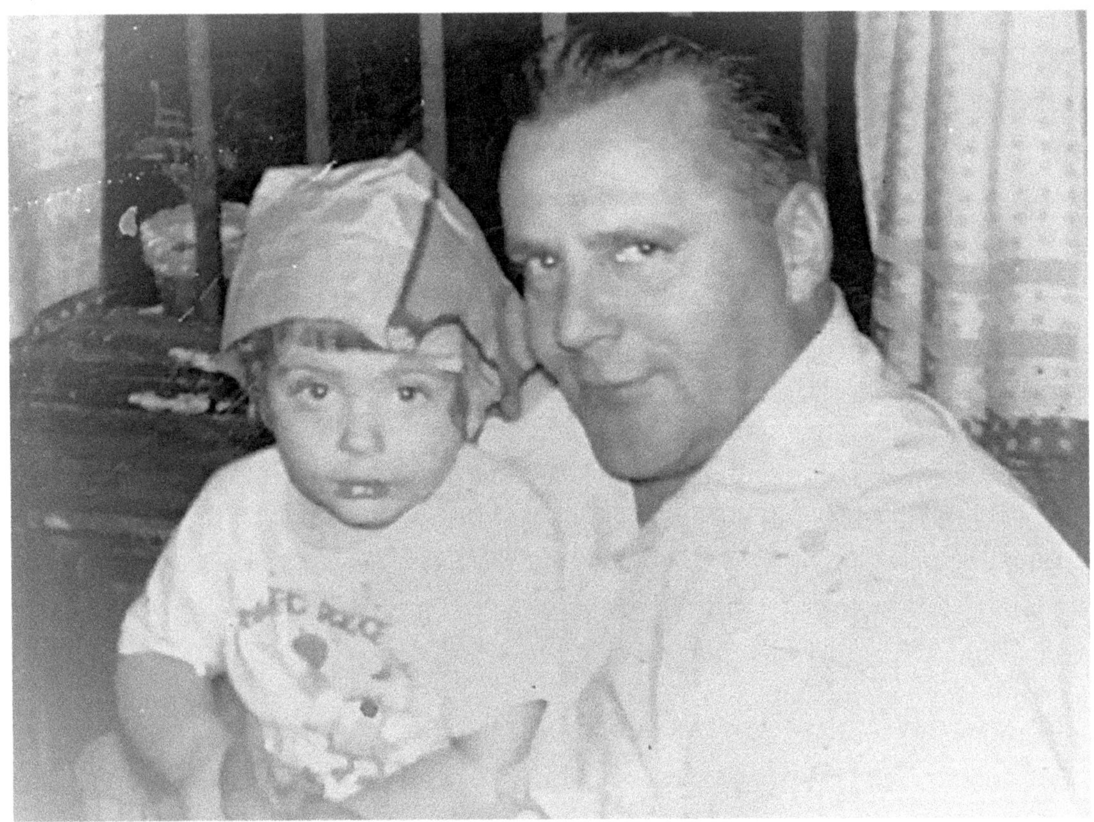

My Daddy, Alfred Robert Blake and myself.
I am wearing my new paper bag hat my Daddy made me.

CHAPTER 12
MEDITATION

Meditation, I try, but these are the times it doesn't really work for me. I do better when I sit in my hot tub and just listen. I have had some very profound moments sitting in that hot tub. There is something about the hot water, the stillness, and the peace, that makes the universe come to me. I often pray in there and I have learned that you need to ask for what you need. But I'll be honest, I don't do anything the way all the books say you're supposed to. I guess I have my own style. It really comes down to listening with my heart and soul and seeking guidance. It seems when I try to force meditation, it becomes a battle and not a gift. The next poem is about one of those times I was trying really hard to connect with my purpose in life, my next step forward, but it wasn't working. So I let go. In letting go, I found a connection.

I Danced With the Universe Today

Sitting in my sacred place,
warm waters all around.
A thought crossed my mind…
and out of the water I bound.

For sunlight blocked my eyes,
and meditation a fight.
Prisms, beautiful pieces of glass,
love to play in the sunlight.

So back I ran to my sacred place,
Magic in my hand.
Hanging up my prism,
I made a magical land.

I played,
with shards of light today,
Rainbow visions…
in full array.

Colors danced upon the water…
caressing my very soul.
Rainbows of light…
healing every hole.

For moments,
I held the universe in my hand.
As it danced upon
my watery land.

I found my body moving,
to each rainbow.
Letting my body,
bask in its warm glow.

I found myself,
in the deepest meditation,
as I played with this,
magical rainbow creation.

I found myself laughing…
not wanting to leave,
the purity of this place,
was hard to conceive.

But I had danced,
with the Universe itself.
I could see and feel,
its immense wealth.

It was not gold,
silver or coin.
There was no price,
to pay or join.

The treasure is…
as it always shall be,
Love itself,
is the magic key!

So if you find Sunlight,
blocking your view,
make yourself rainbows…
dance with the Universe too!

Chapter 13

Finding a Therapist

I did have moments of peace like "I Danced with the Universe Today," but unfortunately, it didn't last. The sadness just kept filling me. I decided to find a counselor, a therapist, someone to help me make sense of my thrashed world. Frankly, just someone to talk to that I wouldn't burden, who perhaps could understand and help guide me through this heartbreaking time in my life. Finding a therapist wasn't easy. It was during COVID and my medical insurance sent me to a cancer survivors group. I didn't go. It wouldn't have helped. I couldn't paint that awful picture I had in my head and share all my pain with people who already had such immense pain of their own. I couldn't hurt them more! I needed my own therapist. In truth, I didn't have any high expectations for him or her. I just wanted someone I could emotionally vomit on, not hurt them, knowing they were getting paid for it. It was their job. They chose it. Not like my poor friends and family. I needed someone to talk to, so I kept fighting for my own therapist. It took a while. COVID didn't make things easy. Finally after two psych evaluations they gave me a list of three names.

One of the names popped out right away. It was a gentleman that used to play soccer with Jimmy. Jimmy thought he was a "ball hog." I laughed silently to myself, "No, Jimmy, don't worry I'm not going to pick him." The next name on the list was a local lady. I thought I'd give her a try. I called the number and left a detailed message about what I needed.

She called back and left a message. It turns out she deals with trauma and felt she could help. She was also a Critical Incident First Responder. To me, that meant I could truly open up and share all the horrors that were still haunting me from when I found my Jimmy, as well as all the fears of being alone again that came back to me from my childhood. I also had triggers that would set off PTSD for me, flashing lights, smells, sounds of ambulances, and so forth.

Our first therapy appointment was over the internet due to COVID. I still thought, "Don't expect too much. Get it all out of you. Dump it on her. You will probably only get to talk to her a couple of times and it will be over."

To my surprise this beautiful woman heard and saw me. There was nothing I couldn't share or that she wouldn't understand. I have been in therapy for over a year now. One of the very first questions she asked me was, "If I could give you medicine to take away your pain, would you want it?" I said, "No," because I knew all this pain was because I loved Jimmy so much. Any type of medicine would only be a Band-Aid. I didn't need a Band-Aid, I needed to learn how to "Walk Through this Fire!" She said, "Then I'm the therapist for you." She was right! It's funny because she doesn't really have the answers I thought she would. She's really full of questions and helps me find my own answers and walk my own path. These next few poems are very intense, but honestly they are some of the most beautiful poems I have ever had the pleasure to write. As my therapist has taught me, "Life is in Layers," lots of layers. In between all the pain, I am blessed. I am grateful. I am a survivor, and I was loved so dearly. My therapist helped me search inside myself, realize the gifts I have been given, and how to not be afraid of them. Often it's more like my therapist has me hold up an invisible mirror. When I ask a question, she will say, "Now that sounds like a good thing for your hot tub!" She has taught me that in my prayers I need to ask for what I need. She is right; I do have gifts. We all do. As this book progresses, I will share a few more experiences and gifts that I have.

Being a foster kid, I had to go to counseling. The counselors were never very good. A woman counselor came up to me on our first and only meeting and in a joking way said, "So you're the crazy one!" Well, I flew out of there! I was a scared teen and the last thing I wanted was to be crazy like my mom, which was another of my fears. Another counselor found my life so fascinating, (after telling my foster father everything we talked about, which is illegal) he wanted to write a book about it. Under hypnosis, I remembered being born. Is it real? I don't know. I didn't feel like I was making it up, but boy oh boy, he found it fascinating. Notice I didn't say he found "me" fascinating. Truth is, I didn't exist to him. I was an interesting subject, but the reality was, I was just a child. I was a scared child and, again, adults were using me one way or another. So, I didn't have much use for therapists, counselors or shrinks, until I met my present day therapist. My advice to you is, if you find the right person, it can work for you too. We do not have to navigate this world alone. What my therapist has taught me is to trust myself, to go within myself in search of the answers I need. My PTSD has gotten better. Not perfect yet, who knows if it ever will be, and yes, I still cry. But I have also learned that pain is an immense teacher, and some lessons can only be taught through unbelievable pain. Life comes in layers.

My heart

Chapter 14
Surrender/Acceptance

Surrender

The fire of pain, unbelievable pain,
licks my very soul.
The agony so deep in truth,
I fear I will never be whole.

I walk through the fire,
to find my way out.
This cannot last forever,
my soul wants to shout!

Put on your big girl panties…
you know how to fight!
Fight my soul cries out…
fight with all your might!

You have battled the Demons
of your past…
Though you are battle weary,
you have the strength to last.

Yet with each day that passes,
you find you've drowned in blood.
The pain is overwhelming,
your soul is drowning in the flood.

You struggle just to breathe…
as the flood of pain pulls you down.
And then a voice cries out…
"Surrender or you shall surely drown."

Fight is all I know…
yet in truth, I can fight, no more.
The flames burn ever deeper,
there is no safe shore.

Slowly I breathe.
I breathe in the drowning fire of pain.
Letting go of the fight,
the fire and I… are one in the same.

I walk in the fire,
breathing in all it has to share.
Knowing once again,
love is everywhere.

Even in these flames of pain,
I can find only "Love" in its wake.
The agony of this pain is "Love!"
It hits me like an earthquake!

"Surrender is the answer…"
this Warrior cries out!
"Become one with the Fire,"
my soul's cry starts to shout!

Find the "Love" in the pain…
and let it heal your wounds.
Fight from the inside out.
Break out of your cocoon.

For you no longer fight with swords…
or a fierce battle cry.
You, my fierce Warrior…
shall learn to reach and fly.

Reach for the heavens,
let your wings fly you there!
It's but a breath away,
if you can dream or dare.

It's a new "Awakening,"
the growth of all I can be.
I reach to the universe,
to see what I can see.

Love envelops me…
I am learning to dance in the fire.
And suddenly the sky turns blue,
and I dance higher and higher.

The lesson learned today;
Love is in all things.
And in my fire I find,
Love has grown me wings.

Love is in all things.
The darkness and the light.
And surrender is in its own way…
A mighty way to fight!

This poem taught me the most about myself. I wanted to fight. I wanted to survive the only way I knew how, and I guess that way for me was denial. I didn't realize it then, how strongly I held onto the hopes and the wishful thinking that this life I was living, without my husband, was nothing but a nightmare, that someday I would wake up. But every morning I woke up, he was still gone. I was still trying to figure out how to deal with that, and the fact that I really was alone again. I have probably said this over and over already, my Jimmy was far from perfect, but he was perfect for me. Whether I liked it or not, he was gone. Though I felt only sadness, not really anger anymore, just unbelievable sadness, I was still in denial.

This is a sign my husband made for me for our anniversary. He always made me something beautiful.

This new life I had, I didn't really want! I didn't know my place in it. All I felt was pain, the searing pain of "Walking Through the Fire." I had a lesson to learn. The fire was there. There was no denying it. The excruciating pain of my horrible loss was in my every waking moment, it was burning me alive. My heart danced between heaven and earth. So, I had a choice. I could sit in the Fire that wasn't going away, or I could pick myself up and learn how to "Walk Through the Fire". In this poem, I describe my struggle of "Walking Through the Fire" and fighting it all the way until the point I could fight no more. I was drowning in the pain, the pain of loss, the pain of loneliness. Then I heard my heart say, "Surrender or you shall surely drown." My heart was trying to tell me this Fire wasn't going away. I had to surrender to the truth of my greatest loss, my Jimmy was gone. I could wallow in the sadness forever and let the flames of pain continue to burn me alive, or I could let the Love, inside all the pain, love me back. When I surrendered, my greatest surprise was, I learned that it was love that really lives inside of all the grief. When I allowed myself to feel only the pain, I was dishonoring the Love that my Jimmy and I had shared. I know it sounds strange, and it did to me too, "Surrender or you shall surely drown." Because when you surrender in a river, you drown and you die! Initially, surrendering to this pain sounded like I had given up the fight. The opposite was true. I had to trust. I had to trust myself. When I did, I learned to fight a different way. I am a Warrior. It doesn't mean I feel nothing. What that means to me is, that despite the battle, despite the pain, despite the humongous mountain before me, I will triumph! I will keep going, one foot in front of the other, even if I have to crawl. That's what it means when

I say I am a Warrior. Quite often the Warrior inside of me is painted in her own blood. She is no hero, other than to herself. She has taken me through many battles in my life, and I know her strength comes from God. There were many times in my life when God and I had words. Yes, I argued with God quite often. I would tell him, "I'm not doing this! I can't do this! Don't expect me to get up and fight again! I'm done!" Then I would be filled with that quiet strengthening peace that I never asked for yet was always granted to my Soul and I would stand up once more, and put one foot in front of the other, and do what I had to do. She is my Warrior.

What I love about this poem most is that it shows my battle and it shows my fear. You can hear the voice of God tell me to Surrender and somehow I trust it, and on the other side, underneath all the pain, when I turn it inside out, all there is is Love. Now this doesn't mean I don't have days when I just cry, but more and more days turn into moments, and I let the layers be what they are, for sometimes my heart is just broken. The difference is, now I can feel all the "Love" inside the pain, the "Love" I was denying myself. Part of it is acceptance, but there is so much more to it than that. "Love" is very powerful and in the end it is the only thing that matters. My heart believes "Love" is the only thing that really survives between our own versions of heaven and earth.

CHAPTER 15
LEARNING THE ART OF SURRENDER

Part 2 of Surrender

The fire and I have merged.
The unbearable pain of death and loss are one.
Now looking at my life,
I see before me, a new one has begun.

Though the unbearable pain
is now more mixed with love,
and I am no longer being buried alive,
it doesn't fit like a glove.

My dreams, my hopes,
my visions, of what I hoped would be…
are only shadows in my mind,
of an old, old me.

The places we would go,
the things we dreamed to see,
are but misty visions
of what I dreamed they'd be.

Now my future
is all in my own hands.
Everything is different,
it's time for new plans.

But I am scared,
I'm alone in my quest.
And I am the one different
from the rest.

My children have plans
and dreams of their own.
And I am frightened
of being alone.

But I need dreams...
and wishes that can come true.
Because I am still living...
though sadly, without you.

Part of me is afraid
I'll die before any dreams come true.
And then I think...
at least I'd be with you.

But the truth is,
I'm more scared to live in a world with no hope.
How do I build dreams
on such a slippery slope?

I find myself afraid
of all that might come to pass.
I fight for everyone else,
but always put me last.

I am a warrior,
for all I hold so dear.
But inside I am a child,
still filled with childlike fear.

I'm running in a circle
going nowhere really fast!
Caught between a future
and dreaming of the past.

It's time I slow down,
and really take a breath.
But the reality is,
I'm scared to death!

What if I can't breathe?
I AM all alone!
Before my Beloved…
it was all I'd ever known.

I am frozen,
in the pain of the past.
And even at age 62,
it feels it will forever last…

You, my beloved…
were more than my home.
You kept the Little Girl in me,
from being left alone.

Now she struggles just to breathe,
her greatest fear, come true.
The Little Girl inside of me
deserves a future too.

Help me stand,
the fear of being alone…
Help me build this child in me…
her forever home.

Help me give her dreams and hopes.
Help me help her stand.
She may never grow up…
this I must understand.

But I can help her feel safe,
loved, and not alone.
Help me be her safe place
she can call home.

Nancy Belle Wood

Chapter 16
The Little Girl

I started recognizing the little girl in me again. The one who had to be pushed aside as a child to deal with grown up things like simply surviving! This Child inside of me had, in a way, become her own person. Though she saw and experienced everything I did, I had no time to lick her wounds or comfort her. I had to be the voice of reason and the protector of my siblings. I had to be the adult! There was no choice. So, I pushed her aside, told her to hide and all would be well. I would protect her too! But the reality of it was, there were times I left and hid, and she had to stay. The Child inside of me suffered her whole childhood one way or another, be it neglect, or physical abuse, rape and even domestic violence between both my real father and mother and my stepfather and mother. As a child we were constantly running away from something or someone. Sleeping in a car or a 24-hour donut place or the Salvation Army shelter. All the while, I felt like the only adult in the situation, and the only protector of my younger siblings. I made sure Santa still came, even waking to find the tree toppled over my passed out stepfather, who had smashed all the presents for my siblings and my mother puffing away on her cigarette sipping coffee with 2 black eyes. Life kept on moving and there was little time to give this Child in me time to heal.

By this, I mean I disassociated myself, my body could not run from what I had to endure but my mind and spirit could. For example, the very first time I was raped, as I was held down in my own bed, hand over my mouth with someone my own mother had put there, I could hear my own mind saying, "The battle is lost, run and hide. We need you strong enough to fight another day." So, the Little Girl inside of me is a Warrior too! But she has scars that need healing and a voice that needs to speak. As my therapist said, "Life is in layers," and this poor child has many layers all her own.

I See You…

I see you…

Tears fill her eyes,
others cannot see.
Pain fills her heart,
though now she is free.

The dreams she had…
all burned up. Now smoke.
She tries to breathe…
but it causes her to choke.

All the dreams,
her little girl had,
All crushed and broken,
She's both mad and sad.

Nothing turned out
as she thought it would.
She tried so hard,
she did all she could.

She struggles to walk.
The future is unclear.
She hears her own heart.
Does anyone care?

Will I ever find peace,
a place I belong?
Has my chance for joy
all but gone?

I see you…
You need not hide our tears.
In truth my friend,
we share the same fears.

Breathe in. Breathe out.
Reach for your life!
You are so much more,
than someone's wife.

Breathe in. Breathe out.
You are not alone.
I too, walk this path with you,
into the unknown.

I am learning to dream again,
to wish and believe.
I'm opening up my mind…
so I may receive.

I have to let go of anger.
It no longer binds my soul.
I try to fill my heart with love…
in this I am whole.

Breathe in. Breathe out.
I do not walk in fear.
Into the future I walk;
the future is unclear.

Know you have a friend,
who can see who you are.
And only wishes you the best…
as you reach for your star!

Little me, in a pink dress.

Chapter 17

Standing Tall

The Little Girl and I are integrating again. I am protective of her, but I have great joy when she jumps out and joins in play. She is a gift to me! If you knew me, you would understand. I LOVE children! I see them, truly see them. Their innocence, their mischievousness. Children and I connect. Children look with their hearts and they see me, a kindred spirit. Their hearts speak to mine. I love them all. Truth be told, I tolerate adults.

Morgan, Jamie and I took a road trip to Yosemite, one of Jimmy and my favorite places. Morgan and Jamie had never been there and I was excited to share with them the beauty of this magical place. On the way there we stopped at a Hot Spring. The water was hot and soothing. In one of the Earths crevices Morgan and I put some of Jimmy's ashes. It seemed a magical place where Jimmy could once again be part of the Earth he so treasured. I was having difficulty taking the little cork plug out of the bottle that held Jimmy's ashes, so Morgan asked if she could help. I told her yes and she popped out her little pocket knife and started working on the cork. Little pieces came out and dropped to the ground. On one of the pieces of cork you could see a little of Jimmy's ashes. Little Morgan says sadly "I dropped Papa." I told her that was fine, Papa wanted to go back to the Earth. After Morgan got the cork off the tiny bottle, Morgan asked me if she could put his ashes in the little crevice we had found with the flowing Hot Spring water. I told her she could and she quickly got to work emptying the small bottle of ashes into the crevice. After she was done we both watched as Jimmy's ashes traveled down the warm water and disappeared into the Earth. Morgan then says "I see Papa!" I thought she meant she could see his ashes, and for some reason I was a little embarrassed and told her not to worry they would disappear into the Earth. Morgan then replied, "No, I SEE Papa!" Morgan then pointed at a small pool of water, made for soaking in the Hot Spring. I looked at her Mom questioningly and she shrugged her shoulders back in response. Morgan then pointed to the pond and said again, "I See Papa!" She looked at both her mother and I as if to say, "Can't you see him too?" Then Morgan said, "I want to swim with Papa." She climbed into the water and sat down with the biggest smile on her face. Sitting across from her was an empty space of water, but it was clear to her Mom and I that she believed she was sitting in the water with her Papa. It was a beautiful moment and one none of us will forget. No I did not see my Jimmy sitting in the water with her, but Morgan did, and it was clear that moment was all for her. She sat there a few minutes, smiled and then climbed out of the water ready to go. She had, had her moment with Papa, there were no tears, only smiles and a giggly silly girl. It was a beautiful thing for her mother and I to see. We have no doubt Morgan had a moment with her Papa and it brought us all great joy.

Children live in the real world; they don't care about fake stuff like adults often do. I call those adults "Plastic People," fake and not living in the real world. I have lived in the real world all my life. The joke with my living five siblings is, I'm a little "Feral!" I raised myself, so I don't know all the unwritten rules of life, the nuances of polite and proper society. I sometimes forget to wash my hands. I believe in the two second rule if you drop something. (Although now it's thirty seconds. I've slowed down a bit!) I don't write thank you notes; they seem silly to me. My hug is all that is needed for a proper thank you! I rub some people wrong, but my heart is honest and loving. So, it is what it is. I like to say I am under construction; God isn't done with me yet! If you ask me, one of my greatest gifts is that I see the children, especially the ones others do not. No one saw me or heard my numerous cries for help as a child. I will not let a child's cry go unheard by me. Nor will I pass up a chance to play with bubbles or dance in the rain.

I Am Proud of You!

Reaching through the layers of my life,
I see her sitting all alone.
The Little Girl inside of me,
longing for a home.

Hello…Can you hear me?
I see you, beautiful child.
I see your dirty face.
A ragamuffin; you look a bit wild.

I see your fierce spirit,
fighting to survive.
I want to thank you;
because of you, we are alive.

You lived in fear,
alone and lost.
Your spirit paid
a heavy cost.

You fought in the darkest of places,
the places no one should go…
where evil lurks around every corner,
it was all you had come to know.

The people who were supposed to protect you
had died, or were broken beyond compare,
and fed you to the Wolves themselves…
as if they didn't care.

You didn't have time to be a child,
to laugh and to play.
The hell you grew up in
had a heavy price to pay.

But you were ready
for the fight.
You held back the demons
with all your might.

They would have your body,
but not your soul.
You told me to hide,
so we could be whole.

You took the beatings
and sexual abuse.
There was nothing else you could do,
to fight was of no use.

Though only a child
this world would see,
I see the mighty warrior…
in me.

I want you to know…
I Am So Proud of You!
You did everything possible,
and all you could do.

I hid that day,
and so many, many, more.
But I saw you…
lying on the floor.

I helped you up,
and together we stood.
I want you to know,
we did all we could.

We protected others.
We grew strong and bold.
Even when there was
only our hand to hold.

Now, we are grown.
But I still see…
the broken little girl
inside of me.

Still beaten,
still broken on the floor.
I'm reaching out my hand and say,
"Little Girl...no more."

You sheltered me
and had me hide.
Now our beautiful heart says,
"Dear One, come inside."

You are the child of my heart,
the one I could not save.
Please dear Little Girl,
don't live in our grave.

You gave all of yourself,
so I may be well.
But I refuse to leave you...
in your emotional hell.

Come into my arms,
let me love away your pain.
Living in this sad space,
you have nothing you can gain.

I know why you hide,
you fear you have nothing left of you.
But that, my silly beautiful child,
it is simply not true!

I have built a safe place,
full of love and bright sunshine!
Where you can feel safe...
any old time.

Take a peek and rest your heart…
I have built this just for you!
You are my foundation…
and I am your shelter too!

This is the very crevice at the Hot Spring, that Morgan put her Papa's ashes in.

This the only picture I have of my mom and dad and the siblings I grew up with. (Right to left) Lower right, that is me. I was the oldest of my mom's last litter of children. Next to me is my sister Lois, sadly she is no longer with us. Behind us is our dad holding the twins, Phyllis and Phillip, sadly my brother and father are no longer with us either. Lastly our mother, Velma, who has also passed.

Chapter 18
Ghosts From the Past

If you're wondering where all this childhood stuff came from, so did I! It's important to note, these poems were kept in the order they were written. I was more surprised than you might be, that in the middle of the worst pain I had ever felt, the loss of my husband, childhood stuff started bubbling out of me. (Stuff I believed I had long since successfully dealt with, or so I thought.)

The loss of my husband threw me for a tailspin. He was my shelter, the strong tree with which I grew, sheltered and protected from having to deal with things by myself. I had never lived alone. I went from foster care into Jimmy's strong and protective arms. I had survived my childhood but was scared to death of ever being alone again. I knew there was true evil in the world because I had lived it. As in every marriage, life was not perfect, but we were committed to each other and did the work and, yes, sometimes it was work to continue to grow together. We knew each other's true hearts and intentions. We raised three children, two girls and a boy. There were extremely difficult times in our marriage, but we held on to each other and weathered life's storms. My Jimmy was solid. I never doubted his love for me, and he never doubted mine for him.

I hate secrets! Secrets were infused in my childhood. Secrets that were never supposed to see the light of day. But to me, they were not secrets or my shame to bare. They were My Story, The Story of My Life, and my survival to become the best me I could be. So, I openly shared my story with friends and people who needed to know they were not alone, that they too could survive because I was proof! I was breaking the chains of the past. I strongly feel that we need to learn from the past or history can repeat itself, and I would not let it happen again!

As I grieved my beloved husband I began to realize I was alone again, my biggest fear. The ghosts from my past started once again knocking on the door to my heart. I am so grateful I was in therapy at this time, because not only did I have no clue as to why I had to deal with everything again, I was emotionally worn out and feared I just couldn't survive this one more time. More and more emotional baggage kept dropping like little bombs blowing up the progress I was trying to make. One step forward, three backwards. (And these were baby steps no less!)

There were times I felt like a puddle and I wondered if I had used up my survivor instinct. Anxiety filled me! I was its prisoner, a shadow of the woman I had been and dreamed of being again someday.

Anxiety

I was born with the strength of hundreds,
not physical strength, but mental.
When the Wolves came knocking at the door,
fight or flight was instrumental.

Sometimes I'd run to protect all I love so dearly.
Other times I'd have to fight, not really a choice, not really.

Fight or Flight was how I was wired, to survive the life I had.
It served me well throughout my childhood, ever since I lost my dad.

Nails on a chalkboard, always on high alert.
Always ready to run, and always hurt.

I was the oldest protector, of all in my care.
Always pushing them forward, from the chasing nightmare.

Sometimes I couldn't run, but my voice pushed them on.
Trying to protect them all, from all that was to come.

I used my strength of hundreds, fighting that awful War.
And now I find my strength has lessened, and I lay on the floor.

Fight or flight, is still how I'm wired.
But I don't have the strength required.

Anxiety is all I feel, and I'm wired to explode.
Sitting on a knife's edge, waiting to implode.

But somehow I know, I'm in charge of me.
I need to recharge and set myself free.

Breathe in. Breathe out. Slow yourself down.
Pick up your pieces. Turn this mess around.

You are not a victim anymore!
Pick yourself up off that dirty floor.

Find your strength and listen to your soul,
Once again, climb out of your hole.

Whatever Wolves come, you've seen them before.
You shine from the inside out. Get up off that floor.

You still live and breathe,
Don't be a dumbass. It's time to believe.

Feel your strength. Let your amber glow.
You are stronger than you will ever know.

The choice is yours, be a puddle on the ground,
or wake up to life's abundance, everywhere, all around.

I'm the fighting Spirit you have inside of you.
I'm here to remind you of all you can do.

Yes, anxiety is real, and you've reasons for it all...
but you are better than this demon and have the wherewithal.

You need to take some time to nurture the scars inside,
and find your strength again, until it's amplified.

Breathe in. Breathe out. The battle is your own.
And trust me Little Warrior, You Are Not Alone.

Chapter 19

Unbearable Sadness

When I started to fight one battle, another one would show its face. It was never ending. The biggest demon I had was my deep, unbearable sadness! I was so deeply sad, it crushed me. I just didn't fit in my own world anymore. Tears fell from my eyes all the time and anytime. Memories flooded my mind and my heart. Holidays brought with them the sadness of the loss of my husband. The empty chair he should have been sitting in, the traditions we had that only he could truly fill. Like reading "Twas the Night Before Christmas" to the grandkids every Christmas Eve, just as he used to do with our three children. I missed Santa too! Jim and I were Santa and Mrs. Claus for many hospitals and organizations. Oh, how I loved loving on all the children! Mrs. Claus died with Santa. Someday she may rise again, but truth be told, I don't think my heart could do it anymore without my other half.

One day I was moping around in the yard, and I heard this voice in my head. It was my husband again, speaking to me as he had quite often. He said he had something to tell me. In a bit of a sassy voice, I told him, "Just spit it out! Say it." He told me he needed me to go in the hot tub and then he would tell me. I was busy. It was the middle of the day, and I had no intention of going in the hot tub. But he wouldn't leave me alone and he kept insisting he had something to tell me. So, I gave up. I got in the hot tub and I tried to meditate, but that proved to be futile. I insisted he just tell me what he wanted to say. I was in the stupid hot tub after all, and yes, I had a bad attitude. I knew it, but the truth is, I didn't care. I explained I was not going to be able to meditate and if he had something to tell me, just spit it out! So very loudly, I could hear him say in my ears, "LIVE! I want you to live!" I said, "Okay Smartass, I'm trying!" He said in a Yoda voice, from Star Wars, "There is no try…There is do or do not!" He was right, of course, but I was doing my best and my best kind of stunk at that moment. It's important to note that we are not always going to be at our best. Some days we are not positive. Some days we wallow in our heartbreak and sadness, and honestly do the best we can to put one foot in front of the other. I think his message to me was that I needed to relax a little, slow down, be kinder to myself, and laugh a little.

It still cracks me up. I literally heard him speak in a Yoda voice! Really? Even in heaven he has a sense of humor. Truth is, all I could do was shake my head. He was right. I needed to keep trying, and I would, one breath at a time. But I needed to learn how to be kinder to myself too. Rome wasn't built in a day, and the pain I was feeling was not going to leave that quickly either, no matter how much I wanted it to. I just had to keep trying.

Sadness

I am sad again...just sad.
Tears keep falling, my heart weeps.
I am alone again,
and my heart knows, it is for keeps.

The rest of this earthly journey
is for me alone.
I must find peace in this body,
it is my earthly home.

But I am "Soul Weary."
My strength is all but gone.
And yet I hear it calling me,
"You must still go on."

But I find myself sitting
in my own pity pit.
Tears keep falling
and all I do is sit.

I am so tired,
and in so much pain,
completely exhausted,
from Life's Learning Game.

I take two steps forward,
and get hit once again.
Always praying
that this is the end.

But the path that's before me
continues on...
and all that's inside me
feels alone and withdrawn.

I'm asking for help,
from all that can.
Light my path
and show me, Who I Am.

I need both rest and strength
I am broken once more.
Sometimes I feel
I am one with the floor.

Can you carry me today,
so my soul can rest?
Or is that asking too much,
and once again I failed the test?

"Everything is wrong, and nothing is wrong,"
I've written that line before.
The only thing that needs to change,
is my perspective once more.

Although I know the answer,
my path is still unclear.
Can I rest a while?
I've had all I can bear.

I know life keeps moving,
I've been running really fast.
And have been fighting
all the demons of my past.

I need some time for healing,
and to catch my breath.
I know I have much to learn
before the hour of my death.

The silence in my house
is deafeningly loud.
And I am so alone,
in a group or crowd.

What's up, is down,
I'm twisted in a knot.
And yet I know I am blessed,
but it's an afterthought.

I feel trapped,
forced to face all my fears.
Staring at the faces
in the distorted mirrors.

I just want to feel safe again,
not huddled in fear.
Is it too much to ask...
for you to hold me near?

I want to feel safe and warm,
sheltered from this storm.
And I believe that if I do,
in the end I'll be transformed too.

Into what? It's hard to say.
But in the end, I'll be okay.

So once again, I plead for rest,
maybe asking, is my test.

I have tried to ask before,
But my mind so jumbled, I asked for more.

I feel you now, I can breathe the warm air.
Thank you for holding me, and answering my prayer.

At this time in my life, I was overwhelmed. Between the excruciating heartache from the loss of my husband and the feelings of being alone, I now felt surrounded by all the demons of my past. I felt like I was in a Hall of Mirrors, the kind that are distorted and are supposed to make you laugh at all the images you see. But laughter was nowhere to be found…It was as if I saw the Devil himself over and over and over. I felt trapped in an endless loop that haunted me, both in my waking hours and the few hours I could sleep. I was mentally and physically exhausted. Though the running I was doing was only in my own mind, I felt like I was in an endless marathon. The Devil pushing me on, faster and faster. I felt the loss of my husband so dearly because he was my shelter and my security. I didn't even realize how much I depended on him in this way until he was gone. It's as if I was a little oak tree that had grown in the shelter and safety of my big oak tree. I had beautiful branches, beautiful leaves, but no roots. The roots I did have were shallow, and the storms of the past were blowing me over, proving to me how alone I was. I needed time to grow roots, to believe in myself, and to learn how to stand alone and be strong, to become the Woman I knew I was always meant to be. I was learning that while I needed the shelter of my beloved husband to grow, I relied on it too much. It was time to find out who "I" was and who "I could be" if I believed in myself. The truth is, I was strong, but I had spent so much time running. I was a fraidy cat. At this point, I was afraid of my own shadow. It was no wonder, after all I had been through. But I was safe now and even though I missed my Jimmy so much, I was stronger than I knew. It was time I started to believe in myself, to grow deep roots.

My beloved

Chapter 20
Lonely

I miss you

I miss you...
I miss everything.
I miss your laughter,
and your voice when you'd sing.

I miss the simple things,
like your kiss on my cheek.
I miss having you near,
when my heart needs to weep.

I miss the sound of your breathing,
in bed next to me...
I miss the way you taught me
a perspective I couldn't see.

I miss your council,
and the simplicity with which you saw life.
I still struggle,
I am still your wife.

The void you left
haunts me still.
You're my other half
and always will be.

I miss you,
Not in a way others can understand.
I know you are with me,
and still hold my hand.

I just miss you so.
You were my best friend.
Someone I thought
would be there till the end.

I see other couples,
and they bring me such joy…
Holding hands as they walk,
I see a love time can't destroy.

I know you walk beside me still,
and kiss me on the cheek.
You grow me flowers everywhere,
your love I'll always seek.

I want what I can't have,
for you are not on this earth anymore.
And I have to wait,
till we walk upon heaven's floor.

Hand in hand we will stroll the clouds,
when once again our souls shall meet…
My heart will once again
feel whole and complete.

You are My One True Love…
the other half of me.
Is it any wonder,
sometimes I just can't see?

I miss you my love,
I know you are but a breath away.
And it is with a grateful heart…
I treasure that today!

I was able to find the space I needed to rest. I slept a lot and watched silly, nonsense shows. I enjoyed getting caught up in other people's stories, just so my heart could rest. I allowed myself the Grace to just be. That was harder than I thought it would be as I could see and feel the pity in other people's eyes. "Poor Dear, shouldn't she be over this by now? How much longer is she going to wallow in this sadness? She just needs to put a smile on her face and keep going. Doesn't she realize she has so much to live for? Poor Dear, she may never be okay! Is she suicidal?" I actually had a friend ask me that once after I shared one of my poems. I want it to be clearly stated, I have never, ever been suicidal. I was done, no joke. I was done. If God were to call me home, I would have been cheering, feeling like I had accomplished all I could in this life and was given the Grace to go home.

This rock is another picture I tried to paint from Pinterest. I was so lonely I felt as if I walked both on earth and in Heaven.

But God wasn't done with me. I could no longer put on the Band-Aid and the fake smile. I was exhausted. I was trying to be everything I was supposed to be, whatever that was. The truth is, my children were having troubles of their own, though they were all grown. I couldn't fix all their stuff either, though my heart wanted to so badly. I understood their pain, they too felt alone. I couldn't walk this path for them any more than they could walk mine for me.

Chapter 21

Lighthouse

This is probably a good time to talk about being a Lighthouse. My therapist, in trying to help me deal with the struggles my adult children were having, tried to help me understand that I couldn't fix their problems, nor was I supposed to. Just as I felt these were my Life Lessons to learn, they too had their own Life Lessons to learn. My therapist explained to me I could be a Lighthouse for them, to help guide them. I thought about that. I had this vision of me as a Lighthouse, strong and impenetrable, tall and out of the reach of everyone, but I had these Wise Eyes shining out to help guide them in the direction they could choose to go. Just like a Lighthouse shows the way to the ships lost at sea. I understood what my therapist was trying to teach me, but I couldn't wrap my mind around being a Lighthouse. For one thing, I didn't feel that wise, like I could really lead the way. That Lighthouse seemed so "Out of reach." I love being close to my family; I didn't want to feel like I had strong stone walls that were unapproachable. I asked my therapist the next meeting, "Would it be okay if I were just me and that my eyes showed the way?" I know it sounds pretty stupid to say it that way, but I explained to her I wanted to be approachable and present, not out of reach. But I did need to learn my boundaries, and how to put up my protective walls when necessary. I couldn't take on other people's burdens, not even my children's. I was working on me. I have always been a fixer. Or as my children would say, a "meddler." Yes, there are times I did butt in where I was not asked to. But looking back at some of the times, I would do it again. It was the right thing to do even if I ended up the bad guy. But other times, it was not my business and I couldn't fix it anyway. They had to learn their own Life Lessons and I needed to let them. My attempts to fix everything were just making me an enabler and no lessons were learned by anyone. My Lesson to Learn in being a Lighthouse, was to tend to my own garden and if possible lead by example and always with Love!

Lighthouse

I cannot walk in your dysfunction.
It is not the path for me.
I cannot make your choices,
they are for you to see.

I have only started breathing,
this new life of mine.
And I only walk in inches
at this moment in time.

So I must step away
from the darkness in your abyss.
I must acknowledge my own demons
or I will be amiss.

Your actions and your choices
trigger all my deepest pain.
And I can't live that life again,
I hold in such disdain.

I want only the best for you,
but that's not what you see.
And I can't seem to change
the distortion you have of me.

You live in your own world of distortion,
where reality is not real.
Where everyone's against you,
and the Victim you only feel.

You are so much more than that,
there is so much more to you.
Step away from the Hall of Mirrors
that block and distort your view.

Love is all I can offer;
You must seek answers on your own.
But when you do, my Dear…
you will find your way back home.

Home my Dear…
is not where you may think.
You can find your home
inside of you, within a blink.

I will try to be the Lighthouse,
standing in the dark.
And if you look inside yourself,
you will find your spark.

Once again a rock I painted from
Pinterest. To me this rock represents
my struggle to find Grace for myself.
The last place I wanted to be was
in my head, but I had to learn the
answers I sought could only come
from inside me.

Chapter 22

Finding Grace for Myself

Slowly, day by day, I tried to treat myself with Grace. Allow myself the space to heal and focus on only me. As a mom who always put her children first, and frankly everyone else too, I found this rather difficult. In some ways, I felt like I was wallowing in my own sadness, but I began to see it as allowing myself the space to "Just Be". My husband and I were big John Denver fans and we would often sing his songs together. There is a John Denver song called "Some Days are Diamonds, Some Days are Stones," which described my days well. Some days went well, some days were rocky. I learned to allow my feelings to have merit. On the hard days, I would ask myself, "Why are you sad today? What specifically made you feel this way today?"

Sometimes I had no answers, but it gave my mind something productive to think about. More often than not, I was able to come up with the reason for my sadness. My therapist would frequently say to me, "Not Right, Not Wrong." At first when my therapist said, "Not Right, not Wrong" I was puzzled, but she was trying to teach me not to be so judgmental of my feelings. I had a right to be sad or happy, or even both at the same time. I had trouble with that in the beginning, because in truth I just wanted to "Snap Out Of It." Something was clearly wrong with me and I needed to "Snap Out Of It". But I learned that was not necessarily the truth, or "My Truth" anyway. I slowly started to learn if I was sad, to be sad. I feared it would last forever, but it never did. I thought if I started crying, the tears would never stop, but they always did. I thought if I lazed around in bed and did nothing, I would never be able to get up again. But I did. I always did. In the state of mind I was in, everything seemed absolute and forever. But it was not.

There was light at the end of the long, dark tunnel. This time in my life reminded me of that country song lyric, "If You're Going Through Hell, Keep on Going!" But to my surprise, "keep on going" didn't mean I had to run. Just as the saying goes, "Stop and Smell the Roses," it is my belief you also have to stop and feel the feelings. You have to feel your pain. I was sick and tired of being emotionally destroyed. I wanted to feel anything but pain! But, like I said a few poems ago, if you turn pain inside out and really look at what the pain is, it is only Love. Yes, Love does hurt sometimes, but it is important to note that the Joy of Love is incredible! Also, there is much to acknowledge when it comes to understanding the painful side of Love. Pain is an incredible teacher. I have said this before and I will say it again. Yes, it hurts to dig deep into your wound, but let's face it, you're hurting anyway, so you might as well dig deep and try to fix it. No matter how much you try to run from this pain, you will never outrun it. It is, and always will be, a part of you. I know this now, and I pray someday you will too…It is a beautiful part of you. I am telling you with all my heart, if you do the work to truly examine what your soul is trying to teach you through this pain, you will not be disappointed.

I believe there is a reason for everything and we are not in charge of what's happening. But we can be in charge of how we choose to handle our pain. May I suggest you go slowly and allow yourself the Grace you need. I fought it, and was so frustrated with myself for not being able to put on those "Big Girl Panties" and just "Suck It Up!" It took time to find this deeply needed compassion for myself. I thought I was doing the "Poor Me" thing, and I would have none of it! I was so afraid I was going to be weak and helpless, the victim, like my mother was. I know now I should have had more faith in myself. I am not, nor have I ever been my mother. When I say I was born with the strength of hundreds, I was; she was not.

So, slowly, I tried putting the broken pieces of my life back together, and it was very frustrating because, again, nothing was happening as fast as I wanted. But I was starting, and that alone was something to be very proud of.

Puzzle

I'm putting the pieces back together of me,
but I'm not the same as I used to be.

Some pieces are broken and glued back together,
Others are lost, or worn from life's weather.

Some pieces are splintered, some shiny and new.
And still some pieces are slightly askew.

I find I can't force them in,
those are places I have never been.

Did I say I hate puzzles? I usually do.
But this puzzle is my life, I must find my way through.

I've got glue and a heart to build on,
one way or another, this is my creation.

I'll shine and rearrange the pieces as I go,
and form new roots as I thrive and grow.

No more "Broken Heart of Pain."
Pick up the pieces once again.

You are an Artist. Use your gifts!
As you create, watch the light shift.

Pick each piece up off the floor.
Pray for guidance and ask for more.

You limit yourself and there is no need.
Catch a ride on a dream, and you will succeed.

You want everything perfect, but that just can't be.
Life is messy. Can't you see?

Put your puzzle together. Go on now. Stop wasting time.
And little by little each piece will shine.

Believe in yourself. You are not alone.
Follow your map; it will lead you home.

Morgan wrote out, I Love You in the rocks. Love is all that matters.

Chapter 23

My Heart's Mosaic

I tried to live again. Find my new normal. I went camping with the daughter of my heart, Jamie, and my granddaughter Morgan. Jimmy and I loved camping and I thought I was ready to do it again. But I really wasn't. I thought I had never been to this camping spot, but I had. It didn't take me long to recognize it. We were camping in almost the exact spot where Jimmy and I camped before. The young family camping next to us played John Denver songs the whole time adding even more memories and pain to my heart. As I looked out my tent window one morning, I said in my heart, "I know we camped here together, Jimmy. I just can't remember the exact spot, but I know it was close." Just then, a Great Blue Heron walked across the campsite next to ours. He was a magnificent bird; Jimmy's very favorite bird to be exact. I just smiled through tears. "I knew the campsite was very close Dear." As you could imagine at this point, I was not much fun on that camping trip. I actually couldn't wait for it to end. I guess I wasn't ready to go camping after all. I felt my Jimmy so close to me that trip. He was happy and he wanted me to be happy. The pain of him not being hand in hand with me was devastating, even with him showing me he walked with me still. I just was not yet ready for that.

I tried to put my broken heart back together again. I had the right idea, but no idea how to do it. No matter how hard I tried, I was not in charge of the hourglass and it was going to take as much time as it was going to take. Frustration, and sometimes even anger, flooded out of me. I was so worn out and tired of being in agonizing pain. In my mind, other people had lost spouses before and seemingly got over it over so quickly. I had been in therapy for over a year and a half and was questioning if it was ever going to end. I was doing the work every week. I was trying to allow myself Grace and the time I needed. Yet every week it seemed to be something new. If it wasn't the loneliness, then it was how quiet the house was. I tried to get myself involved in different groups. Some worked, some didn't. But, I kept trying. I kept myself busy with different projects, volunteering in different ways. Despite several attempts, I still didn't feel like me. I knew I would never be the same again. But, I also held onto the belief that there was a place in this world where I could feel more like me, even if it was a new me. It didn't have to be a sad me. I wanted so much to be able to genuinely be happy again, to have a purpose, a reason for my life. I knew I was blessed with many gifts. The question my therapist asked of me, "What are your gifts?" often came back to my heart and mind. I started taking inventory of who I was, and more importantly who I wanted to be. These limits were self-imposed. I had the choice to reach for the stars. So I did, and I reached with all my heart.

My Heart's Mosaic

One by one, I put each piece back in place,
Trying to cover all the bloody space.

Some have jagged edges, being torn too many times…
Others are misshapen, perhaps in other lifetimes.

But this heart is worth repairing…gently with grace,
for each piece holds the answers, for the human race.

For I have been learning, and treasure each piece,
and at the end of time, I will be my masterpiece.

So, it's time to shine it up, and tend to it with care,
for deep inside of it…you will find me in there.

This is not a race, but should be a labor of love.
For I am not alone and I'm watched over from above.

Patience is a gift, not often one of mine.
But as one tends a garden, I must tend this heart of mine.

Pulling out the weeds of doubt…
so all the love can again sprout.

Hold fast to my compass, for my journey is long.
I will need this heart, to sing my new song.

You can do it! You can shine once more!
Shine from the inside out, not shattered on the floor.

You are an Artist, and your heart is your gift!
I know the pieces will not all magically fit.

But fear not, you will know where they go.
And with each piece you put in, you will grow.

Now get to work, but take your time,
and make my beautiful heart shine!

This rock I painted from Pinterest, represents to me my self reflection
and the beginning of realizing I have gifts aplenty.

My Mosaic Heart

Chapter 24

Owning my Gifts

Some of the things I'm saying might sound strange to you. I used to worry more about what people thought, less so now. While talking to my therapist, quite often I would say, "Oh, this is going to sound strange" and she would say, "Just say it. Own it." So little by little, I started to listen with less of my head and more of my heart. I learned to embrace my gifts. Always believed that God sent me (all of us) with everything I needed to deal with this life. They were my gifts. When the right time came, I would open them. Slowly, I started opening the beautiful gifts of my Soul. I had always realized that I could feel other people's pain and block it when necessary. I learned to read people's moods and develop those skills when I was a child. I learned very young to trust my gut. Bad people still raise the hair on my body. It was one of my survival skills and came in quite handy as I grew up. As an adult, I could tell if someone liked me or not. I could tell when they were hurting and if there was something I could do to help. It's like their heart spoke to me.

But I'll be honest, I didn't listen to it a lot. Mostly, I minded my own business and took care of my family. I tried to be an average, everyday good mom and wife. With the passing of my husband, I found my heart reached for the heavens and felt closely connected. I always had an unusual connection when it came to my Poems. They often bubbled out of me with a wisdom I never felt I myself possessed. My poems were as much a gift for me as they were for anyone who needed them. I could always tell by someone's response if my Poems spoke to them. If, when I was finished reading my poem, the person listening said, "Oh, that's nice," then they didn't hear a thing. My poems are many things, but not "nice".

Once I complained to my sister that the Poems just kept bubbling out of me at the most inconvenient times, like when I was driving. I told her, if I didn't pull over, and write something down right away, I felt like the wisdom in the message would be lost forever. My sister suggested that I get a little handheld tape recorder to use in the car. Pull over, blurt out my poem, and write it down later. Sounded like a good idea, so I tried it. One of my best poems came to me in that exact situation. I pulled over, got out my little recorder, and blurted out this poem. It was a great poem, but even when I was recording, I sounded like I was spaced-out or something, like I wasn't me. Later when I was sitting down to write what I had recorded, the voice on the recording scared me. It sounded nothing like me. Scary is one thing I don't do, so I couldn't record any more poems. I was back to pen and paper.

It is my belief that after my husband passed, the space between heaven and earth was very thin between us. He spoke to my heart all the time. We joked. We laughed. He held me when I cried. There was a time though, that I couldn't hear him anymore. It broke my heart. I missed him so much. But it turns out this was a crucial time of my healing. I had different work to do. As I sat in the hot tub trying to meditate, different things would come to my mind. When meditation seemed out of reach, I would pray out loud. Often my prayers and thoughts would end up in a different direction than I thought they would. But, I had learned that I was safe and in the loving arms of heaven itself. So I trusted these times; I could learn the lessons my Soul needed to teach me. To my surprise, one time I relived my first rape, moment by moment. I had just turned thirteen. At the end of reliving this nightmare, I found myself standing in the hot tub, tears streaming down my face, with my arms reaching up to heaven. Slowly, my eyes opened and what I thought had been a few moments had been forty-five minutes! I felt exhausted emotionally and physically. Why did I need to relive this now? I just couldn't see the benefit of adding to my current pain. But in the end, I needed to listen with my Soul, and I had.

Another surprising time while in the hot tub again during my attempt at meditation, my stepfather came to me. Just so you know, he's dead. I heard him ask me for forgiveness. I laughed out loud! I could not believe he was asking me to forgive him. His nickname for me was El Diablo, The Devil. He was every bit the Devil in my life as he was in the lives of others. I don't believe in hell, but if there is a hell, he would be there. Instead, my mind thought he must not have learned any lessons this life has to offer, and so if God listened to me at all, he sent him back as an amoeba! Yep, he had to start all over again, he was that bad! Here he was now, in my mind, asking me for forgiveness? Well I learned a long time ago giving someone forgiveness is more for me than for them. But still, that was a big ask! When I realized he was being sincere, and that he deserved a sincere answer back, I stopped to think about it. The only answer I could come up with was that I could forgive him for what he'd done to me, but it was not my place to forgive him for what he had done to anyone else. He needed to ask them himself.

Little by little, and ever so slowly, I was addressing all the demons of my past, all over again. Even the ones I thought I had dealt with long ago. It felt like this time, I was addressing them more on a Soul level than on a human level. I was reaching out with my very Soul and trying to heal my broken mosaic heart.

The more I reached out from inside me, the more my senses grew. I was unwrapping more of the gifts God sent me with. One day, there was a man walking across the street. I had seen him many times before. He looked lonely but was persevering. To his and my surprise, I yelled across the street to this man I have never spoken to before, "I see you! I just want you to know I see you!" I was shocked and so surprised at what had come out of my mouth. This poor man would surely think I was crazy. To my surprise and great joy, he walked across the street to me and I repeated myself, "I know it sounds strange, but I just wanted you to know I see you! I don't know why I had to tell you, but I just did!" and I gave a little shrug. I had to own it now, there was no hiding from myself that day. To my heart's joy, this stranger wrapped his arms around me and gave me a genuine hug! It felt like it came from his very Soul to mine, and yes, for those of you wondering, this was during Covid, but neither one of us thought of it in that precious moment. I have had other experiences similar to this where I was guided from something deep inside of me. The difference now is I embrace those moments and I keep trusting my gut. Some people ask me, "How do you know it was okay to approach them?" The answer is, I would know if it was not. Sometimes the person may not know their Soul called me, but if their Soul didn't call to me, I wouldn't know to go to them. I feel a Soul reach out to me and if my Soul hears their call, I must respond. I do not think I have any more wisdom than anyone. I just know I'm not afraid to talk about the elephant in the room or share my emotions. If you knew me you would understand, I simply have no choice.

I personally love this rock I painted, from Pinterest. Look at it, what do you see? People see many things, it really needs you to study it. Some see a butterfly, other lighting, or branches. Look deeper. For me it is my husband and my energy forces meeting face to face. Can you see it now? I hope so. Not all things can be seen with our eyes, you must use your heart.

Chapter 25

A Child of Light

I Am a Child of Light

All my life, I have had to fight,
fight for the privilege of my life.

I battled the demons of abuse,
endured when fight was of no use.

When my world crashed all around,
I picked myself up off the ground.

First one step and then another,
I cut the chains that pulled me under.

I wiped the filth from my body,
determined I would be somebody.

Each step I took, I learned to stand taller,
not be imprisoned in that squalor.

I didn't know it then, not in words anyway,
I was a Child of Light and I would shine one day.

Deep inside, I could hear her say,
"You are not alone, I am here to stay."

But I had lessons to learn, and a life to live.
And my "Soul of Light" had much to give.

I could hear her talk to me,
Offering guidance and clarity.

But I was busy surviving this life,
and often it cut me, like a knife.

So much this life has taught me, and at great cost!
I struggle again, not to get lost.

But when I listen to Her voice, she shouts!
"I Am Enough For Me!"
And when I open up my mind,
A Child of Light is what I see!

I hold on to her message, and let it fill my soul.
My Higher Self and I are once again whole.

But I can't walk in the clouds,
my job is here on earth.
I have been sent here to learn lessons,
since the day of my birth.

The difference now, can't be denied.
She and I walk side-by-side.

We dance together, side by side…
There is no denying, she is my guide.

She knows I have a job to do,
And she has promised to see it through.

And I have learned not to push Her away…
She teaches me more, everyday.

I Am a Child of Light, and I will let my Love shine.
This Love is a gift from the Divine.

So keep the lessons coming; I've got this now,
and if I don't, She will teach me how.

For She is the best of me,
the Light of God for all to see.

A Child of Light? Where did that come from? It came to me as a gift of "Knowing," for lack of a better way to explain it. I have shared with you how my poems just bubble out of me. I am as surprised as anyone else when I hear my poem for the first time. It's like getting a message and I am taking dictation. Writing this poem was a lot like what my therapist had been trying to teach me, "Just own it." This poem was me claiming who I was. Believing who I was. Seeing who I was.

I Am a Child of Light! Though this may sound silly to some, it brought me peace. We are All Children of Light. I don't mean like a light bulb; I mean energy. When I speak of my Higher Self, it means my Wiser Self. The me who has been around, for only God knows how long. The me, who has learned lessons probably for lifetimes. I know She is wise, She is kind, and She is made of only Love. In truth, I always knew She was there. But I didn't have time or the belief in myself to truly put my faith and belief in her. Now, there will be many of you who think I'm just nuts. It may sound silly or crazy, but for me, it is just touching the part of me that God and I have always been working on. My very Soul. I must admit, putting it in words and trying to explain the unexplainable part of myself, isn't very easy. I guess that's why I started this out by saying, it's a "Knowing." My Soul is in the same place all my poems come from. I have been connecting to that part of me my whole life. She is really no stranger to me.

The day I wrote this poem, "I Am a Child of Light," I felt like I was glowing from the inside out. It felt like I was shining. A peace filled me, a calmness that I haven't had in quite a while. Alone didn't seem so alone or overwhelming. I was healing! Healing the wounds of my past and the loss of my great love. No, he doesn't walk on this earth anymore, but his footprints cover my heart and my Soul. I will walk with him again, when it is time, but for now I have things to do.

I do not believe in coincidences and I often see little "God Winks," messages, gifts from God and my loved ones who have passed away. It could be a song or a thought, but it is how He shows me He is close to me and I do not walk alone.

I still have life to live, and so many reasons to be grateful!

Chapter 26
Back to School

I have walked through the Fire, I have had to take emotional inventory of all that I am. I have asked myself the hard questions, and listened to the even harder answers. I have learned to accept that most things are beyond my control. The few things I can control have to do with me and no one else. I find I am often using the beautiful gifts that were given to me at birth, even the new ones I just recently unwrapped. I don't know what life has in store for me, but I'm not afraid anymore. It is my belief that even with God watching over us, we are filled with free will and choice. That is why we have our own lessons to learn, so we may choose to be the people worthy of this beautiful life we are given.

This next poem "Battle for your Soul" is especially meaningful to me. In many ways it represents all the lessons I have learned in this lifetime.

Battle for Your Soul

You asked me, "Why? Why now?"
The answer is, "Why not?"
You have survived "Hell" itself...
and your very soul has fought!

Fought to stand. Fought to breathe.
Fought to stay alive.
And now you are free,
but still struggling to thrive.

Your Survival came at a cost,
a cost you had no time to pay.
You were too busy running...
just surviving, day to day.

Now you are free,
but it's time to pay the cost.
That's why now,
you feel so lost.

See, believe it or not,
you're stronger than you know.
Your heart says it's time,
and it will go slow.

But you must recognize
the damage done to you.
It's like going back to school.
You must pay your due.

The Lessons Learned from pain,
are the ones that cost your soul.
But when you learn them,
one by one, you will again be whole.

Running from the truth,
just causes more pain.
The lessons will repeat,
and leave a new blood stain.

Let the layers unveil themselves,
a tear at a time.
Yes, it can seem endless,
Dear Friend of mine.

Deal with each layer
that will reveal as you go.
If you're sad... be sad...
only you will know.

Do the work.
Repay your debt.
And in the end,
you'll be amazed at what you get.

Your heart will open,
even more than you could guess.
And yes, you won't feel…
frankly, such a mess.

You learn patience…
with your own heart.
And what a beautiful place,
to start!

And true kindness,
starts with you!
A peace will fill your heart.
It feels like magic too!

The journey is painful,
of that I cannot lie.
But to do anything else…
is in itself, to die.

Do the work, and yes, it is work,
the hardest you have ever done.
But in the end…
the freedom of your soul is won!

Debt paid, Lessons Learned.
The soul you were meant to be reborn.
Piece by broken piece,
you mended what was once torn.

You are whole again,
not broken on the floor.
You are in control of you,
not anyone else! No more!

You got this. Be brave.
You already won the battle!
This is just the time you learn,
from all that had you rattled.

You're going back to school,
The school for your soul.
And I promise you, if you do the work…
you will come out whole.

I love you. I see you!
I promise you're in there.
And I have walked that walk…
and I am always here!

You are not alone.
When you fall, and you will,
We can lock arms together…
and climb that awful hill.

Be patient with yourself.
You have been through hell!
So, listen to the lessons,
your Soul has learned so well.

Chapter 27

The Backside of a Waterfall

I am hoping that this book will help light the way for anyone going through indescribable pain and grief. I know I personally felt like I just had to deal with it, keep going, one foot in front of the other. But I felt like a sighted person who suddenly lost their vision. I was blind. I could not see a path before me. All I could feel were the Flames of Pain torturing my body and Soul to the point where I felt I could hardly stand or walk one more step. I knew I was in pain because I loved so deeply. What I didn't know was how to survive one more day. When you are in such horrible pain it becomes all-consuming. That saying "You can't see the forest for the trees," is very true.

Why was I hurting so much? LOVE. Simple, beautiful, LOVE. The poem "Surrender" was really a game-changer for me. Many of my friends wanted me to change the name to just about anything else. To them it sounded like I was giving up, even suicidal. But it was everything but that. It was as simple as breaking down why I was hurting. I was hurting because I LOVED with all my heart. I was hurting because of LOVE. Well, then, what is LOVE? It is the most beautiful and precious gift we have. To feel with our entire being. The gift of Love is the very Breath of Heaven. In the poem "Surrender," I dissect "LOVE." I turn it inside out. I Surrender to all the pain and beauty of Love. I allow myself to get swallowed up by the pain of my deepest heartbreak and once I am completely submerged in the "Pain of Love," I realize I still live. I open my eyes as if under the water. I see "LOVE" in all its beauty and splendor.

Yes, there is still pain. How could there not be? But I also see the gift of "LOVE" in all her beauty. It's like looking at the backside of a waterfall. It is still beautiful, just a different view. I believe this is the day I truly accepted what happened. ("Surrender" was written over a year after my husband's death.) I thought I had accepted my husband's passing, but I was fighting it. I knew he was gone, but my heart was still in denial. By surrendering myself to the Pain, I realized a few things. One big thing was, I survived! The other was "OUR LOVE" was still beautiful even through the goggles of pain. I would not change any of it! Every tear I shed for the rest of my life over this devastating loss will always be worth it! I was loved, and I loved with all of my being. In that I was truly blessed. As the mat on my front porch says, "Beyond Blessed."

This Love had taught me so much about myself, about the world, and about how I want to be in this world. I could be a Lighthouse, a Guide. If I could help anyone on this journey, if my poems touched anyone's heart and helped in any way so they could feel less alone, I was using the gifts I was given, and honoring the Love my husband and I had for each other.

It is my deepest wish as I reach out my hand and my heart to you, that you not feel alone, that you learn to trust yourself. You are stronger than you know. Be the sunshine you wish to see in the world. Be your own Lighthouse. Be true to who you are, even as you are beginning to learn, own it. Be proud of yourself. I believe in you. Put one foot in front of the other. Take my hand; we can walk together. Anything is Possible. There is beauty even on the other side of a waterfall. We are all, Beyond Blessed.

It is now almost three years since my husband's passing. I have graduated (my words) from therapy. Yes, I still miss my Jimmy with all my heart. But I can tell you he is proud of me. I am embracing this new path my life is on. Recently a lady I know said to me, "You look good!" I smiled back at her and said, "I am good!" She replied, "You're glowing! Are you in love?" I giggled, and answered, "No! Well maybe…with myself!" I was a little embarrassed as the words came out. We both giggled! Why is it such a strange thing to say that? But then I thought, Own it!

In the end…Pain is an incredible teacher and Love is all that matters.

Your Friend, Nancy Belle Wood

My dear friend, Leslie, took me to see this amazing tree she found on her morning walk. She was so excited to share this treasure she had found. She told me to look inside its trunk, and to my surprise the large base of the tree was hollow. The tree had only its outer walls to support it, yet it survived and still thrived. It was tall and had branches and leave on top, despite the odds. It was a survivor. Leslie then said, "Its like you, Nancy. Even with the childhood you had, despite the odds against you, you not only survived but you thrived." Wow! I am so blessed. Oh and yes, Leslie is a Ya Ya.

Jim gave me this beautiful gift for one of our anniversaries. He carved our names in a heart and our wedding anniversary date.